CW00796785

The Essential Guide To
Touring Bicycles

Written by Bicycle Touring Pro - Darren Alff

The bicycle featured on the cover of this book is the Co-Motion Pangea touring bicycle. The colors shown on the top and bottom of the book cover are all of the colors available to you when you choose the paint for your Co-Motion touring bicycle.

www.co-motion.com

Introduction

Welcome to the wonderful world of touring bicycles!

Hopefully you've obtained a copy of this book because you want to learn about bicycles made for either short or long-distance bicycle touring and you want to use the information inside this book to help you find your perfect bicycle touring vehicle.

Over the course of this short book you will learn about the basic features, parts and terminology you should know about when looking at touring bicycles. You'll also receive some tips for when and where to purchase your new touring bike, and you'll receive instructions on how to use this book to find the touring bicycle that best fits your needs.

The information in the first part of this book is detailed enough to teach you about the basics of touring bicycles, but I've left out all the boring, overly-technical details that put most people to sleep and are usually best reserved for professional frame builders and touring bike designers.

In the second half of this book you will find a large collection of touring bicycles made by both large and small companies from all across the globe. On each page is a new bicycle, shown with its name, company name, description, price and a link to the manufacturer's official website.

The bicycles featured in the second half of this book are broken up into five main categories (Commuting, Sport Touring, Light Touring, Road Touring and Off-Road Touring) and are listed in alphabetical order by their company name, followed by the name of the bicycle.

Before we get into the specific touring bicycles, however, it is important that you first have a basic understanding of what exactly a touring bicycle is and how this specific type of bicycle differs from the road and mountain bike models you are likely familiar with.

About The Author

Darren Alff is the founder of www.bicycletouringpro.com, the world's most trusted bicycle touring resource for beginner, intermediate and experienced bicycle travelers. With more than 1,000 free articles, interviews and videos about bicycle touring currently available on the website, Darren now has more than 500,000 individuals from all around the world looking to him for the advice, inspiration and how-to information needed to conduct a bicycle tour of any length.

Darren is also the founder of www.gobicycletouring.com - a fun and stylish website that allows you to quickly and easily find the best guided and self-guided bicycle tours on the planet.

Darren Alff went from being a 17-year old high-school kid, riding across America on a decrepit old mountain bike, to the *Bicycle Touring Pro*, after having bicycled across North America six separate times and cycling across dozens of different countries all around the world. Now he's teaching others about the secrets to bicycle touring success!

His how-to bicycle touring book, *The Bicycle Traveler's Blueprint* has sold thousands of copies all around the world and is considered to be the definitive guide to self-supported bicycle touring. *The Bicycle Traveler's Blueprint* is truly a step-by-step bicycle touring guide, handed to you on a silver platter.

In addition, Darren is the author of two other popular cycling books:

- *Stretching for Cyclists*
- *Winter Cycling*

To learn more about the author, be sure to visit his popular bicycle touring websites at www.bicycletouringpro.com and www.gobicycletouring.com.

Table Of Contents

What Is A Touring Bicycle?

There are a number of different features, characteristics and extras that make touring bicycles unique when compared to other bicycle models.

In general, a touring bicycle is a type of bike that is specifically designed to handle the demands of bicycle touring.

An individual partaking in a bicycle tour is typically (but not always) traveling for more than one day and carrying a considerable amount of clothing, food, gear, water and other items on his or her bicycle. For this reason, most touring bicycles are designed to be comfortable, stable, strong and capable of carrying heavy loads.

Special features found on many touring bike models include:

- ⋏ A frame design that favors comfort, stability and utility over speed.

- ⋏ A long wheelbase (which means that the wheels on a touring bicycle are further apart than on traditional road or mountain bike models. The reason touring bikes are designed with a long wheelbase is because such a design is more comfortable on your body and the extra length ensures that your feet and legs don't hit the equipment you are carrying on the back of your bicycle as you pedal).

- ⋏ Heavy duty forks and wheels (to help support the extra weight that touring bikes need to carry).

- ⋏ Multiple mounting points (for front and rear racks, water bottle cages and fenders or mudguards).

- ⋏ And the ability to carry (with the assistance of one or two bicycle racks) either two or four panniers (which are bicycle-specific bags that attach to the racks of your bicycle, so that the weight of the gear you need for your tour is placed onto your bicycle's frame, rather than onto your body (as would be the case if you tried to carry everything you needed for your bike tour in a backpack like a long-distance hiker)).

The bicycle above is a traditional road touring bicycle without accessories.

Below is the same touring bicycle, mounted with both front and rear racks.

Here's the same touring bicycle again, this time with racks and fenders.

Finally, the image below shows a "fully-loaded" touring bicycle with racks, panniers, fenders and water bottles.

Some (but not all) touring bicycles also:

- ⚓ Use standard parts and metals, which makes them easy to repair while out on the road and in foreign countries.

- ⚓ Have handlebars that allow for multiple hand positions (which is important on long bike rides, because your hands can fall asleep and suffer from nerve damage if they remain in the same position for too long).

- ⚓ Have saddles that are more comfortable than those found on many road or mountain bike models.

- ⚓ And come with a wide-range of gears (especially low gears), so as to help you climb long, steep roads while carrying a heavy load.

Every touring bicycle is a little different and each has been designed with a specific type of bicycle touring in mind. The goal of this book is to help you find a bicycle that is in your price range, available in your country and designed for the specific type of bicycle touring that you wish to participate in.

However, before we go about selecting your perfect touring bicycle, it is important that you have a basic understanding of the different types of bicycle tours that are available to you, as bicycle touring can mean a number of different things, and the type of touring bike you ultimately select is going to very much depend on the type of bicycle tour in which you plan to participate.

This is very important, so let me say it again. The type of touring bicycle you need to purchase will depend on the type of bicycle tour in which you plan to participate.

This means that the first step in finding your perfect touring bicycle is to decide which type of bicycle tour you plan to conduct. After you've figured that out, finding the appropriate touring bicycle becomes a whole lot easier.

The Different Types Of Bicycle Tours

To understand the different types of touring bicycles, you must first have a basic understanding of the different types of bicycle tours.

There are three main types of bicycle tours (Guided, Self-Guided and Self-Supported), and more than a dozen different sub-types.

The Guided Bicycle Tour

A guided bicycle tour is a type of bicycle touring in which you pay to be escorted along a pre-designed path by an experienced bicycle touring guide or company, and your belongings (such as your food, clothing, toiletries, etc.) are carried in a vehicle that meets you at various checkpoints along your route.

Guided bicycle tours range in size from 2 to 20+ people, with tour participants often times coming from a number of different countries all around the world.

Support and personnel vary by tour and tour company, but one guide typically rides with the group on his or her bicycle each day, while a second tour guide drives a support van carrying your luggage. Larger tour groups may have as many as three or more guides working to escort you along your route each day. In addition to carrying your belongings from one point to the next, the support van provided by the touring company also makes it possible for tour participants to bridge less attractive and/or more challenging sections of a route, if need be.

While bicycles used for the duration of the trip may or may not be included in the tour's overall cost, most tour operators will provide you with a bicycle of some kind if you choose not to bring your own (although the cost for renting a bicycle from the company may be extra). Most tour companies will also provide you with a comprehensive packing list, route/mapping details, and an information package containing details on the sights you can expect to see along the way, cultural highlights and scenic stops (although the extent of information varies from company to company).

If you enjoy traveling with a group, meeting new people, riding with an experienced bicycle touring guide and having a structured daily schedule, then a guided bicycle tour is probably the best fit for you. The guides will point out places of interest, organize activities and excursions, and are there to help in case of mechanical, mental or physical breakdowns.

With all the tour details sorted for you and almost everything paid for in advance, guided bicycle touring allows you to simply show up for the start of the tour and enjoy the ride!

The Self-Guided Bicycle Tour

A self-guided bicycle tour is similar to a guided bicycle tour in that the route, lodging and meals have all been taken care of for you by an established bicycle touring company. The difference, however, is that on a self-guided tour you will not be joined by an experienced bicycle touring guide. Instead, you must navigate a pre-designed course on your own, while carrying whatever belongings you might have with you on your bicycle (although some self-guided bicycle tours will transport your luggage each day from one hotel to the next).

While a guided bicycle tour is typically conducted with a large group of people, self-guided bicycle tours can be done alone or with a group of almost any size.

While meals may or may not be included with your tour, bicycle tours of this type are generally far less expensive than guided bicycle tours (because you aren't paying for a guide to accompany you along your route). Self-guided bicycle tours also offer more freedom to stop and smell the roses (or take a detour, if you so wish) along the way.

If you choose to conduct a self-guided bicycle tour, you should consider your level of comfort with navigating through a different country, communicating in a foreign language, reading maps and signs, ordering food, and dealing with flats or other minor emergencies. While some tour participants would rather avoid these types of situations, others will find these challenges to be an enjoyable part of the bicycle touring experience.

If you're looking to participate in a relatively inexpensive bicycle tour where all (or most) of your tour details are taken care of for you in advance, but you want the freedom to choose your own travel companions, cycle at your own pace and come up with your own schedule each day, then a self-guided bicycle tour might be in your future!

The Self-Supported Bicycle Tour

Finally, there is the self-supported bicycle tour, which requires you to travel alone (without a guide) and carry all the clothing, tools, and gear you need to survive for days, weeks or months on end.

While your food, route details and lodging are all taken care of for you in advance by a touring company on both guided and self-guided bicycle tours, self-supported bicycle touring require you to figure out all of these details on your own – either in advance or once you get out there on the road.

By far the least expensive means of traveling by bike, self-supported bicycle touring requires the most amount of planning, preparation and skill. Knowing how to navigate, find food and water, interact with locals, repair and maintain your bicycle, ride in all types of traffic (while carrying a heavy load) and secure lodging for the night are all important skills that the self-supported bicycle tourist must posses.

Despite the education that is required to successfully conduct your first self-supported bicycle tour, this type of touring continues to be one of the most popular means of traveling by bike.

In addition to these three main types of bicycle tours, there are also a number of different bicycle touring sub-types and alternative names.

Day Touring

Day touring isn't really a type of bicycle tour at all, but actually just a single-day bike ride. There are two main types of day tours you might encounter:

Day touring can consist of simply jumping on your bicycle and going for a ride that stretches for a span of 24-hours or less. This might just be a long bike ride near your home, a road trip where you travel by car and then spend part of your time cycling, or it could involve renting a bicycle in a foreign city/country and taking a spin around the local area.

The other type of long day trip you might encounter is a bicycle tour conducted by an organization which brings cyclists together in a single location and these people ride their bikes for a relatively long distance in a single day. Typical rides of this type can range from 10 to 100+ miles/kilometers in a 24-hour time span and are often times organized as an event that you have to pay to be a part of.

While traditional bicycle touring is typically an overnight activity, these single-day bike rides and organized cycling events are often times called "bicycle tours."

Day touring can be conducted as either a guided, self-guided or self-supported bicycle tour.

S24O or Overnight Touring

The S24O (or Sub-24-Hour-Overnight (also referred to as "Overnight Touring")) is a type of bicycle tour in which you spend one day riding your bicycle to a nearby destination (a friend's house, campground, hotel, etc.) where you rest for the night and then spend the following day returning by bike to your home or starting location.

This is slightly different than day touring because the S24O consists of two days of cycling and one overnight stay, whereas a day tour consists of only one day of cycling and no overnight rest stops.

S24O bike tours are typically self-supported.

Credit Card Touring

Credit card touring is when you travel by bike and pack almost nothing but the clothes on your back and a credit card (or cash) to buy things along the way. Instead of carrying a tent and sleeping bag, you pay to sleep in a hotel each night. Instead of carrying a camp stove and cooking your own food, you buy food along the way. Credit card tours are typically (but not always) less than a week in length and are usually not supported by a touring company.

Audax

Audax is a style of long-distance cycling most popular in France, but also seen quite frequently in Holland, Belgium and Germany. The term is now also commonly used to describe a different style of long-distance cycling event found in countries such as France, Great Britain, Singapore, Australia, Canada and the U.S.A.

The original form of the Audax style involves riding in strict group formation at a steady pace set by a road captain. The group attempts to maintain a pace of 22.5 km/h between stops. The route is pre-planned with designated stopping points. For longer Audax events the group may ride between 16 and 20 hours in a day before stopping at a designated sleeping location. The goal of the Audax is to finish inside the prescribed time limit with all members of the group present. A support vehicle is allowed to follow each group of riders.

In some countries such as Australia and Great Britain, the term Audax is also used for Randonnees. These are also long-distance bicycle events, but riders are free to cycle at their own pace, stop or sleep wherever they want and form groups randomly, provided they stay within the time limit.

Randonneuring

Randonneuring is a type of organized long-distance bicycle riding, with rides typically covering between 100 and 1,200 kilometers (60-750 miles). A participant in this particular kind of bicycle riding is known as a randonneur and an event of this sort is called a randonnee.

Randonneuring is not a competitive sport. It is a test of endurance, self-sufficiency and bicycle touring skills. All riders who complete the task are congratulated and no prizes are given to those with the fastest times.

Randonneurs are expected to carry poor weather clothing, spare parts and tools. Rides in excess of 300 kilometers frequently involve night riding and require lights, spare bulbs and reflective gear.

Light Touring

Light touring refers to a type of bike tour in which you carry just a small load of food and equipment on your bicycle – usually in two panniers mounted on the rear rack of your bike. While light touring can technically be guided, self-guided or self-supported, light touring differs from fully-loaded bicycle touring (which we will discuss in just a moment) because a loaded bicycle tourist will be carrying his or her belongings in four total panniers (two on the front and two on the back), while a light tourist will only have two panniers (usually mounted on the rear rack of his or her bicycle).

Ultra-lite Touring

Ultra-lite bicycle touring is a name that can be attached to almost any type of bicycle tour. Ultra-lite touring simply refers to a means of bike travel in which measures are taken to drastically reduce the size and weight of food, clothing and equipment so as to increase speed and the overall distance covered.

Ultra-lite touring is typically, but not always, self-supported.

Supported Touring

A supported bicycle tour is any type of bike tour where you receive assistance from either a private individual, tour guide or touring company in carrying your gear and/or navigating along your route.

If you sign up to conduct a guided bike tour with a professional touring company, you are signing up to participate in a supported tour. If you choose to participate in a self-guided bicycle tour, you may or may not be participating in a supported bike tour – depending on whether or not the touring company you've booked with will be transporting you and/or your belongings from one destination to the next.

Supported touring differs from guided bicycle touring because a guided tour is always conducted with either a professional guide or a touring company, whereas a supported tour may be (but is not always) supported by a friend or loved one driving alongside you in a chase vehicle.

Guided Self-Supported Touring

A guided self-supported bicycle tour is a type of tour where you are required to carry everything you need to survive on your bicycle (food, clothing, bike tools, etc.), but a guide from a touring company leads you along a specific route. With these types of tours, you typically ride with a small group of people and are then escorted on a daily basis by an experienced bicycle touring guide.

As its name suggests, guided self-supported bicycle touring is a combination of guided and self-supported bicycle touring. There is usually no support vehicle on a tour of this type.

Bikepacking / Cyclocamping

Bikepacking and/or cyclocamping refer to a means of bicycle travel in which you cycle mainly off-road and carry a minimalistic amount of food, gear and clothing. Because of the rough terrain involved with bikepacking/cyclocamping, mountain bikes and/or off-road friendly touring bicycles are commonly used.

While bikepacking and cyclocamping refer largely to the same thing, the major difference between the two activities is that bikepacking is more about the bike riding experience, while cyclocamping is more about getting into nature on your bike and finding a pleasant place to camp. One puts more emphasis on the cycling and the other puts more emphasis on the camping.

Bikepacking/cyclocamping is typically a self-supported endeavor.

Mixed-Terrain Touring

Mixed-terrain touring is a name that can be applied to almost any type of bicycle touring. While most bicycle tours are conducted on paved roads or bicycle paths, a mixed-terrain bicycle tour might require you to cycle across dirt roads and/or trails, snow covered passes, ice-laden tundra, or anything in between.

Mixed-terrain touring can be guided, self-guided or self-supported.

Expedition Touring

Expedition touring is sub-sect of self-supported bicycle touring. The main difference between the two, however, is that expedition touring requires you to travel through remote areas, developing nations, and/or places outside of traditional bicycle touring roads and routes, while traditional self-supported bicycle touring is usually conducted on paved roads and in civilized countries.

Loaded Or Fully-Loaded Touring

Loaded bicycle touring (also called fully-loaded bicycle touring) refers to any bicycle tour where you are carrying four or more panniers on your bike. A loaded touring bicycle usually consists of two large panniers on the rear rack and two smaller panniers on the front. A loaded bicycle might also be equipped with a handlebar bag, rack pack(s), and/or additional gear on it's front or rear racks.

If you choose to carry only two panniers of the rear rack of your bicycle, you are conducting a light bicycle tour. But if you have four panniers on your bicycle, you are riding fully-loaded.

Traditional Bicycle Touring

When you hear someone talking about traditional bicycle touring, they are generally referring to a fully-loaded, self-supported bicycle tour on paved roads using a road touring bicycle.

Traditional bicycle touring is the type of bicycle tour most self-supported bike tourists will participate in when they first start out. These individuals may eventually transition into off-road touring or other, more challenging types of bicycle tours, but most self-supported travelers start out as traditional bicycle tourists.

Bicycle Travel

While bicycle travel may refer to any of the various types of bicycle touring, it is generally meant to refer to someone who travels by bike for long periods of time (typically for months or years on end).

Bicycle travel refers to a type of bicycle touring that it not just a short term trip by bike with a beginning and an end date, but a means of long-term travel. You might choose to call yourself a bicycle traveler after you've been on the road for several months or years. Or you might decide that you have become a bicycle traveler after frequent bicycle touring excursions have become a regular part of your life.

Bicycle travel is a self-supported endeavor. However, a bicycle traveler may, at one point or another, choose to participate in a guided or self-guided bicycle tour during his or her travels.

* * *

As you can see, "bicycle touring" can mean a number of different things. A bicycle tour can be a one-day event, a week-long journey near your home or a multi month-long adventure spanning the globe.

A bicycle tour can be guided, self-guided or self-supported. You may find yourself cycling on paved roads, established bicycle paths, or in remote regions of the world where dirt or gravel roads/trails are common.

Because there are so many different types of bicycle touring, there are several different types of touring bicycles. Each type of touring bicycle has been designed to handle the demands of a different type of bicycle tour.

As you will see in just a moment, finding your ideal touring bicycle will depend greatly on the type of bicycle touring you wish to conduct and, the amount of money you are willing to spend to find your perfect touring bike, and (in some instances) the type of touring bicycles available in your region of the world.

What Kind Of Bicycle Tour Is Right For You?

The trick now is for you to decide exactly which type of bicycle tour you wish to participate in, because the type of touring you wish to conduct will ultimately dictate the type of touring bicycle you need to purchase.

Stop reading for a moment and really think about this. What kind of bicycle tour do you want to go on?

- Do you want to be able to use your bike for short day trips near your home or long, fast rides with your local bike club?

- Do you want to take guided tours where your gear is carried for you in a van and you are free to simply ride your bike without carrying all that extra weight?

- Do you want to travel by yourself, but pack light and ride as fast as possible?

- Do you want to cycle off-road in remote corners of the world where paved roads and established bicycle paths are few and far between?

- Do you want the experience of loaded bicycle touring, but with the added safety that comes from traveling with an experienced guide?

- Or do you want to hit the open road with your bike in tow and all the gear you need to survive on your own for days, weeks or months on end?

If you can decide right now which type of bicycle touring you are most interested in, you'll have a much easier time finding your perfect touring bicycle.

The Different Types Of Touring Bicycles

With so many different types of bicycle touring available, it would be almost impossible to design a single bicycle that was perfect for each of the aforementioned types of bike travel.

What this means is that every touring bicycle you encounter has been designed with a specific type of bicycle touring in mind. Some of the bikes are built for short day trips; others are built for fast group rides and racing; and others are manufactured for round-the-world travel.

When it comes time for you to look at the bicycles listed in the second half of this book, you will see that each bicycle is listed in one of the following five categories:

- ⋏ Commuting
- ⋏ Sport Touring
- ⋏ Light Touring
- ⋏ Road Touring
- ⋏ Off-Road Touring

The following pages will help to summarize each of the five main types of touring bicycles.

Commuting

Bicycles in the Commuting category are designed for short trips around your home. They aren't designed to go particularly fast, carry especially heavy loads or give you very many hand positions. These bikes are great for trips to your local supermarket, office or locations within a relatively close distance to your home and they can be used for short overnight bike tours as well, but they aren't designed to take you around the world or get you where you want to go in any sort of a hurry.

Sport Touring

Bicycles in the Sport Touring category are designed for speed. These types of bicycles look as though they might be road racing bicycles, and many of them can be used in exactly that way. Unlike traditional road racing bicycles, however, Sport Touring bicycles have some kind of touring capabilities. Many Sport Touring bicycle, for example, have braze-ons that allow for front or rear racks and many of them can handle the demands of lightweight (credit card or ultralite) bicycle touring.

Light Touring

Light Touring refers to bicycles that have been designed to be more comfortable on your body and at the same time support a small amount of weight. Many of these bicycles come with rear racks, fenders and all of the characteristics you would expect to see on a full-fledged touring bicycle, but they just aren't equipped for carrying super heavy loads on long-distance, round-the-world adventures.

Road Touring

Bicycles in the Road Touring category are designed for long-distance bike touring. These bicycles are capable of mounting front and rear racks, carrying large loads and getting you across entire cities, states and countries. Road Touring bicycles are designed for bicycle touring on paved roads and, while some of them can handle a fair amount of off-road riding, they are usually best kept where the pavement is flat and smooth.

Off-Road Touring

Finally, Off-Road Touring bicycles have been designed to go anywhere and do just about anything. These bicycles are built to be ridden on dirt and gravel roads, single-track trails and other non-paved surfaces. These types of bicycles usually (but not always) have 26" or 29" mountain-bike wheels and tires that are better suited for off-road riding. While bikes of this type are capable of traveling on paved roads as well, off-road conditions are where touring bikes of this type really excel.

* * *

Please note that many touring bicycles may technically fit into more than one touring bike category. In order to keep things relatively simple, however, each bicycle inside this book is listed under only one category (the category that best describes how the bicycle is meant to be used).

How To Determine The Type Of Touring Bicycle You Need

As was previously mentioned, the first step in finding your perfect touring bicycle is to decide which type of bicycle tour you plan to conduct. Will you want to use your bicycle for:

⅄ Day Touring?

⅄ Guided or Supported Touring?

⅄ Audax, Randonneuring or Credit-Card Touring?

⅄ Lightweight Touring

⅄ Self-Supported or Fully-Loaded Touring?

You then need to determine which category of touring bicycles is most appropriate for the type of bicycle tour you wish to participate in.

Will you be using your bike for:

⅄ **Commuting?** (Day Touring, Overnight Touring, Light Touring)

⅄ **Sport Touring?** (Day Touring, Supported Touring, Credit-Card Touring, Audax, Randonneuring)

⅄ **Light Touring?** (Supported Touring, Credit-Card Touring, Overnight Touring)

⅄ **Road Touring?** (Light Touring, Overnight Touring, Self-Supported or Fully-Loaded Touring)

⅄ **Off-Road Touring?** (Bikepacking, Cyclocamping, Expedition Touring, Mixed-Terrain Touring, Self-Supported Touring, Fully-Loaded Touring)

This is the most important step in finding your perfect touring bicycle.

With each bicycle designed for a slightly different type of bicycle travel, you need to decide right away which of the five main touring bicycle types listed above, you are going to need for your specific type of travel.

Do You Really Need A Touring Bicycle?

Maybe you already have a road or mountain bicycle in your garage at home and you're thinking to yourself, "Do I really need to buy a new bicycle just to participate in a bicycle tour?"

The answer to that question is somewhat complex and depends on a number of factors.

It depends, for example, upon:

- What kind of bicycle tour you wish to participate in.

- How long you plan to be on the road.

- What kind of bike you currently have.

- What kind of condition your current bicycle is in.

- Where in the world you plan to travel with your bicycle in the future.

- What the road conditions are going to be like on your travels.

- How much gear you plan to carry.

- How comfortable you wish to be on your bike as you are riding.

- The amount of money you are willing to spend.

- And a whole host of other factors.

The truth is, however, that you don't always need a touring-specific bicycle in order to participate in a bicycle tour.

For short bike tours (anything less than a week in length), almost any type of bicycle will do. But the longer you stay on the road, the more miles/kilometers you plan to cover and the more gear you wish to carry, the more important it becomes to have a proper touring bicycle.

There are two major downsides to using road or mountain bike models for long-distance bicycle touring.

First of all, because most road and mountain bike models are not meant to be ridden day after day, for hours on end, using them on a long bike tour may cause you to experience back, neck, shoulder, arm, hand and/or groin pain problems. The lack of hand positions on mountain bike models, especially, has been known to cause serious (even long lasting) nerve damage with some touring cyclists.

Secondly, the lack of braze-ons for front and rear racks on most road and mountain bike models mean that you will be unable able to carry the amount of gear necessary for long-distance bicycle tours. Instead, you will be forced to carry any additional equipment that you might need for your travels in a trailer that you pull behind your bike (a perfectly viable option, but usually not as ideal as using a set of racks and panniers) or a set of specially-built racks that are designed to be used on front, rear and full-suspension mountain bikes.

If all of this seems confusing, consider the following scenarios:

Let's say you want to conduct a series of long day rides near your home. You don't plan on carrying a lot of gear with you and you plan on returning home at the end of each day so you can sleep in your own bed at night. You have a perfectly good road bike in your garage at home and you're wondering if that old bike will work for the type of "bicycle tours" that you are planning to conduct.

In this particular situation, you can almost certainly get away with using your current bicycle. In fact, purchasing a new bike for short one-day bike rides near your home would almost certainly be a waste of money.

Let's say, however, that you're planning a different type of bicycle tour.

This time, let's say you want to conduct a week-long credit card tour with a friend. Together, the two of you are going to cycle 350 miles across your home state, stay in hotels each night and eat at restaurants along the way. Once again, you have a perfectly good road bike you are thinking of using for the tour, but you aren't sure if the bicycle is up to the demands of lightweight credit-card touring.

In this scenario, like the last, your current road bike will likely suffice. While your road bike may not be the most comfortable bike to ride on a 350-mile bicycle tour across your home state, it will probably work just fine (especially if you can attach a rear rack to the bicycle so you can easily carry with you the small amount of food, clothing, toiletries and personal items you will likely need for your journey.)

A more common scenario, however, goes a little something like this:

Let's say that you want to do some major bicycle touring. You're planning a month-long bicycle tour across Europe, during which you plan to camp in a tent at night and eat out at restaurants along the way (thus reducing your weight a bit by not carrying a camp stove or excessive amounts of food). The thing is, you have an old road bike at home and you're hoping you can save a little money by using your current bicycle for this month-long cycling adventure.

The danger in using a road bike for loaded bicycle touring (outside of the previously mentioned comfort issues) is that most road bikes are not designed to carry excessive amounts of weight and their frames may crack, bend or break under excessive loads.

By using an old bicycle (or a bicycle not designed for the rigors of loaded tour- ing), you risk not only significant damage to your bicycle, but significant harm to your body as well (especially if your bicycle frame breaks apart while you are riding it).

While your current road bike may work in a situation such as this, I would think seriously about purchasing a touring-specific bicycle.

In fact, my suggestion in almost any scenario is that if have any doubts about whether or not your current bicycle can be used for loaded bicycle touring, you should probably consider investing in a proper touring bicycle.

Now let's look at one final scenario:

Let's say that you're planning a bicycle tour in which you plan to camp and cook your own food. You might even be planning to do a little off-road cycling and you've got a perfectly good mountain bike at home. Wanting to save a little money, you're hoping you can use that old mountain bike for your up- coming bicycle adventure.

The truth is, mountain bikes (especially the kind without front or rear suspension) are the one type of bicycle that are probably best designed as an alternative to a proper touring bicycle. They are strong, built to take a beating, have low gears that help you climb steep terrain, and many hard tail mountain bike models come with braze- ons, which allow you to mount a rear rack and panniers (at the very least).

That said, however, mountain bike designs tend to cause three major problems for touring cyclists.

First of all, the shape of the frame and additional features found on most mountain bike models can cause a lot of discomfort for bicycle travelers. Not only are mountain bicycles not designed for long hours in the saddle, but the flat handlebars found on most mountain bike models fail to offer many hand positions, which can cause a lot of pain (and even nerve damage) in your fingers, hands and arms as you ride.

Secondly, a mountain bicycle with either front or rear suspension is not de- signed to be used with traditional bicycle touring racks. Without a set of bike racks, you will have to be creative when it comes to carrying the gear needed for your travels.

There are, however, some workarounds to this problem. If you decide you want to use a mountain bike for bicycle touring purposes, you can choose to carry your gear, not with a set of racks and panniers (as it typical with a traditional touring bicycle), but in a trailer that you pull behind your bike. (In fact, in many off-road scenarios, a trailer can be better to use than a set of racks and panniers).

Another option for carrying your gear on a mountain bike is to purchase a set of full-suspension mountain bike racks. While traditional bicycle touring racks will not work on a front or full-suspension mountain bike, these special types of racks can be mounted on almost any type of bicycle - regardless of whether or not the bike has front, rear or locked suspension.

Finally, mountain bikes are slower than their road and touring bike counterparts. The large, treaded tires you find on most mountain bike models are great for off-road scenarios where the wide tires and deep tread helps the bike to grab at the earth beneath it. But in on-road scenarios, the wide tires and deep tread found on mountain bike tires does nothing but slow you down, decrease your efficiency on the bike and make it harder for you to pedal.

As you can see, the process of deciding whether or not you actually need a touring-specific bicycle can be quite complex and depends on a number of different factors.

If, after reading the rest of this book, you still have questions about whether or not you really need a proper touring bicycle, you can contact me for assistance by leaving a comment on the following web page:

http://bicycletouringpro.com/blog/really-need-touring-bicycle/

Be sure to read through the previous comments on this page before leaving a comment of your own. In most cases, you will likely find that your question has already been answered by someone in a similar situation.

Metals Used In Touring Bike Frames

Because of the weight that touring bikes need to carry and the amount of time you will spend on the bike while traveling, the material used in making the frame of a touring bicycle is extremely important.

Of all the touring bike models in the world, there are four main metals used in the construction of touring bicycle frames:

- Steel

- Aluminum

- Titanium

- Platinum

Each of the four metal types has various benefits and drawbacks.

Steel

Strong, flexible materials like steel have been a favorite amongst touring cyclists for a very long time. In the past, almost all touring bicycles were constructed using hi-tensile or cromoly steel. Even today, most of the touring bicycles on the market are constructed with some kind of steel frame.

Steel is a great material for building a touring bicycle because, while it may be a little on the heavy side, a steel frame can support a large load; is flexible, and therefore relatively comfortable on your body; and is easy to repair, if necessary, while on your travels.

Without getting too technical, most of the steel alloys that are used in producing touring bicycle frames have the same general stiffness and weight. When you start to look at the specific types of steels used in touring bicycle frames you begin see the same names used over and over again.

For example: Reynolds 531, Reynolds 653, Reynolds 725

Unless you are one of those people who love to obsess over minute details, I wouldn't worry too much about the different types of steels that you encounter. All you need to know is that each of these steel types is ever so slightly different because the manufacturer of these types of steel tubes have added chromium and molybdenum particles so as to increase their strength and decrease their weight. By adding these materials to the steel, it allows the tubes to be thinned out in the middle, which makes the frame (and the overall bike) that much lighter.

Because of these extra particles that are added to the steel to make them stronger, steel bike frames tend to have much more slender tubes when compared with the tubes of aluminum framed bicycles. By having more slender tubes, the flexibility of the frame is increased, and this makes for a more comfortable riding experience. It may seem like a small detail, but flexibility and comfort on a long-distance bicycle tour is extremely important, so a touring bicycle built on a steel frame is a great way to go.

In summary, steel alloy frames are strong, tough, comfortable, relatively light- weight, affordable, and easy to repair just about anywhere in the world. That's why steel frames are so popular in the manufacturing of touring bicycles.

Aluminum

Aluminum is the second most popular type of metal used in touring bicycle frames. An aluminum frame is lightweight, responsive, rust proof and affordable. Unlike steel, however, which is flexible and relatively heavy, aluminum is both stiff and lightweight.

Aluminum is less dense than steel and because of this, the diameter of aluminum frame tubes are increased so as to provide additional support. This over-sized tubing results in a light, but rigid (and sometimes uncomfortable) bicycle frame. While many cyclists appreciate the lightweight frames that aluminum bicycles provide, the stiffness of an aluminum frame can feel a bit harsh to some touring cyclists.

Titanium

Titanium is an excellent frame building material due to its strength and light weight. However, it is quite expensive due to material and fabrication costs.

The strength of titanium as a frame material is comparable to steel, but a stiff titanium tube will have a larger diameter than comparable steel tubing. That said, the two main advantages of titanium over steel are its light weight and its resistance to corrosion. While titanium does make for a great touring bicycle frame, the excessive cost of the material will be limiting for many prospective touring bike owners.

Platinum

Platinum, like titanium, is another high-end metal used in the construction of bicycle frames. Platinum is a material that many associate with fine jewelry, but it is a material that is commonly used in bicycle frames as well. Much like titanium, platinum has an incredible resistance to corrosion and high temperatures, but it is expensive and is therefore a material usually only found in high-end bicycles.

It should be noted that bicycle frames made of platinum are not 100% platinum, but usually a combination of platinum mixed with steel.

* * *

The frame of your bicycle is the heart of your machine. The components (i.e. derailleurs, shifters, brakes, etc.) can be changed and upgraded over time, but a weak, heavy or uncomfortably stiff frame will remain with you no matter what. This is why selecting the right frame material for your bicycle is so incredibly important.

Parts, Design & Geometry

The frame geometry of a traditional touring bicycle is designed for long hours on the road. A touring frame differs from other types of bicycles in a number of ways. These differences allow for:

⊁ A more stable ride while carrying heavy loads.

⊁ More sensitive steering.

⊁ A lower center of gravity.

⊁ And a more comfortable, upright riding position.

Every touring bicycle has a slightly different design, but when you look at most touring bicycles, you will see basic parts that look a little something like this:

The frame of a standard touring bicycle essentially consists of three main triangles. One side of the main triangle is formed by the seat tube, which tilts back a little from the vertical position and into which the seat post holding the saddle fits.

The top tube extends forward from the seat tube, usually at a horizontal (or nearly horizontal) angle, while the down tube runs at an angle from the front of the frame to the bottom of the seat tube. At this bottom juncture, the two main tubes connect to the side of a short piece of larger-diameter tubing in which the axle for the pedal and crank assembly turn. This short piece of tubing is called the bottom bracket.

At the front of the main triangle, the juncture at the top and downtubes usually is truncated slightly where it connects with another short, larger-diameter tube called the head tube, in which the assembly holding the handlebars and front wheel pivots. The fork holding the front wheel is attached to the steering tube, which pivots inside the head tube. The stem that holds the handlebars is inserted into the top of the steering tube and is clamped with a wedging device.

Two rear triangles made of smaller-diameter tubing extend on either side of the rear wheel. Each connect at the lower front with the bottom bracket and uses the seat tube for a third side. The lower tubes are called chainstays and the upper ones are the seatstays. The axles of the wheels clamp into the fork ends at the ends of the fork and the dropouts at the lower back junctures of the rear triangles.

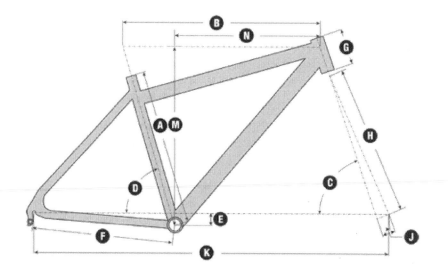

When looking at the geometrical measurements of a touring bicycle, the following data is often times collected and shared by bicycle manufacturers:

A - Seat Tube Length

B - Top Tube Effective

C - Head Tube Angle

D - Seat Tube Angle

E - Bottom Bracket Drop

F - Chainstay Length

G - Head Tube Length

H - Fork Length

J - Fork Offset

K - Wheelbase

M - Stack

N - Reach

When it comes to frame design and geometry, things can quickly become incredibly complex.

Your bicycle's design determines how comfortable you are on the bike, how the frame itself handles the distribution of weight and how the bike handles in general. For example, your bicycle's frame plays a large part in whether or not you can ride your bike in a straight line with your hands lifted off the handlebars.

The frame design also determines how sharply your bicycle can make turns and whip around corners. A touring cyclist, however, usually doesn't care about this, as he or she is going to be riding in a much more casual and relaxed position, where sharp turns and fast corners are not a common occurrence.

As a bicycle traveler, you want a bike that handles with ease. You want to be able to ride the bike while looking at the passing scenery and not have to be constantly worrying about keeping your bike in a straight line.

Because of the way most touring bicycles are configured, the manufacturer of your bicycle has a limited number of variables to work with and alter. For example, the differences in frame angles among various bicycle designs are minimal. The angle of the seat tube, for example, might be 74 degrees on one bicycle frame and 72 degrees on another. The average person would be unable to tell the difference between the two.

Most of the measurements recorded in your bicycle's frame geometry are dictated in large part by your size and other frame building limitations.

For example, the length of the seat tube cannot be increased more than a small amount, because you have to be able to reach the pedals when you are seated and you want to be able to put your feet on the ground when you are in a standing position.

There are a few variables that the builder can change, however. These variables include the angles of the seat tube and the head tube, the fork rake (the distance produced by the forward bend of the fork), the length of the chainstays, the length of the top tube, the length of and angle of the down tube and the height of the bottom bracket from the ground.

When you move or alter one of these variables, that alteration affects the geometry in another part of the bicycle.

In the end, the design of your touring bicycle is best left to the professionals.

You should, however, know that the standard diamond-shaped frame found on most touring bike models has proven for several decades now to be the best construction available for its weight.

For women who are considering the purchase of a touring bicycle, you should typically avoid a mixte (or women's) frame, as these types of designs are not nearly as strong as those of the standard type. However, the mixte frame design found on many touring bicycles can be used for commuting and light touring purposes.

What Size Bicycle Frame Do You Need?

While the geometry of specific touring bicycles differ from one model to the next, the most important factor to pay attention to is the length of the seat tube. The seat tube the frame tube that runs from the bottom bracket (the part of the frame around which the pedal cranks revolve) and your seat cluster (which is the junction between the seat tube, the top tube and the seat stays of the frame).

When we talk about frame size, we are talking about the distance between the center of the bottom bracket and the top of the seat tube. This measurement is usually (but not always) listed in either centimeters or a corresponding scales of standard measurements (such as XS, S, M, L, XL, XXL).

The most common touring bicycle frame sizes are: 44 cm, 48cm, 52 cm, 54 cm, 56 cm, 58 cm, 62cm, and 64 cm.

It is not necessarily uncommon to see other sizes (such as 49 or 57 cm).

Many touring bike manufacturers will list the recommended frame size based on your specific height. But the easiest way to find the proper size bicycle is to stand over a bicycle with your legs on both sides of the bike. You should be able to stand over the top tube and have both feet comfortably rest on the ground with about one or two inches between your groin and the top tube. If you stand over the bicycle and the tub tube hits your crotch, the bike is too big for you. On the other hand, if you stand over the bicycle and there are three or more inches between your crotch at the top tube, the bicycle is likely too small.

While many of the high-end touring bicycle companies will go out of their way to help you find the right size bicycle frame for your body type (and may even design a custom-fit bike if you really need something special), one of the best ways to get fit properly for a touring bicycle is to go to your local bike shop and have them assist you. Some bike shops will simply have you stand over bicycles of various sizes, while others with more sophisticated technology will place you on a specialized piece of equipment designed to find the best fitting bicycle for your specific body type.

You don't want to get a bicycle that is too large or too small, so selecting the proper frame size is incredibly important to the comfort of your ride, your ability to pedal effectively and your overall handling of the bike itself.

Bicycle Touring Wheels

In much the same way that there are different types of metals used in touring bicycle frames, there are also different types of wheels used on the various types of touring bicycles.

700c Wheels

The 700c wheel is the most common type of bicycle wheel you will see and it is used on many different types of bicycles—from racing, to cyclo-cross and even touring bikes. The advantage of a 700c wheel is that it rolls more easily than wheels with a smaller diameter.

While road and cyclo-cross racers want a 700c wheel that is light and aerodynamic, the touring cyclist wants a 700c wheel that is rigid and strong. 700c touring wheels are different from 700c racing wheels in that they weight more, usually have more spokes than a racing wheel and are built to support a wider tire capable of handling the additional weight that touring bikes need to support.

700c wheels are a popular choice for cyclists traveling in large, modern countries. Cyclists in North America, Europe and Australia are usually the main buyers of touring bicycles with 700c wheels.

26 Inch Wheels

26-inch wheels are the most common wheel size for off-road touring bicycles. The typical 26-inch rim has a diameter of 559 mm (22.0") and an outside tire diameter of 26.2" (665 mm). One of the advantages of 26 inch wheels is that the rim and tire combination allows you to run lower tire pressures for better traction and shock absorption without dramatically increasing your risk of puncturing the tube.

26 inch wheels are a popular choice for touring cyclists who plan to travel around the world or cycle in remote corners where bike shops are few and far between. This is because 26 inch wheels and tires are a standard wheel/tire size all over the world, whereas 700c wheels and tires are not.

29 Inch Wheels

29-inch wheels (which also conform to the popular 700c wheel size) are becoming more and more popular. Their popularity started in the cyclo-cross world, but has recently crossed over into mountain biking and touring as well. The 29 inch wheel's rim diameter of 622 mm (24.5 inches) is identical to most road, hybrid and touring bicycle wheels, but they are typically reinforced for greater durability in off-road riding. This large wheel size and its added durability is seen as a plus by many, but 29 inch wheels/tires are still a hard-to-find commodity in many bike shops around the world, so they should be used with a fair amount of caution.

20 Inch Wheels

When it comes to folding bicycles and recumbents, the small 20 inch wheel often times reigns supreme. These types of wheels are a popular size on BMX racing bicycles, but they are also suitable for use on bicycles made for young and small riders. In addition, their size makes them stronger to withstand the additional loads generated by jumps, stunts and loaded touring. And because they have a small diameter, they have a reduced rotational inertia, which makes for easy wheel acceleration. 20 inch wheels, because they are used on children's bicycles, are also very easy to find just about anywhere in the world.

Hubs, Spokes & Rims

Bicycle wheels are made up of three basic parts: the hub, spokes and rim.

The Hub

The hub is the center-most part of a bicycle wheel. It consists of an axle, bearings and a hub shell. There are a number of different types of bicycle hubs, as you will see in just a moment. The hub is usually made of steel or aluminum and may sometimes consist of both metals at once, with steel commonly being used in the axle and bearings, and lightweight aluminum being used for the hub shell.

The Spokes

The spokes are a series of thin metal rods that radiate outward from the hub shell toward the rim of your wheels. The spokes, believe it or not, are what actually hold your bicycle wheels together and support both you, the weight of your bicycle and any additional gear you might be carrying.

While many bicycle wheels consist of 32 or 28 radiating spokes (and some racing bikes can be found with as few as 24 spokes or less), most touring bike wheels are equipped with 36 spokes. The fewer spokes you have on your bicycle, the lighter your bicycle will be, but the less weight the wheels can support. This is why touring bicycle wheels tend to have more spokes than many road and mountain bike models. The added number of spokes helps to increase the wheel strength, allowing you to carry more gear, while only slightly increasing your bicycle's overall weight.

The Rim

The rim is the large metal hoop on the outside of your wheels, onto which your spokes and tires attach. If your bicycle uses rim brakes to bring itself to a stop, then your rims will consist of a smooth parallel braking surface, whereas rims designed to be used with disc or hub brakes may not have this smooth outside surface.

Most touring bicycle rims are made of aluminum, because aluminum is both light and strong. However, some bicycle rims are made of steel.

Rohloff Hubs

Rohloff hubs combine the traditional bicycle hub with the common (and less expensive) derailleur gears found on most bicycle models. In essence, the gears on a Rohloff hub are located inside the hub itself, rather than on the outside, like traditional bicycle gearing. Rohloff hubs are more expensive than competing gear systems and are usually only found on high-end touring bike models. Rohloff hubs usually take some time to break in and get used to, but they are robust and sought after in the touring world due to their reliability and ease of use. Replacement parts are extremely difficult to find.

Dynamo Hubs

A dynamo hub (or hub dynamo) has a small electrical generator built into the hub of wheel that allows the spinning motion of the wheels to power small electronic items, such as lights, cell phones and other digital devices. Like Rohloff hubs, Dynamo hubs are expensive and usually only seen on high-end touring bike models. Few touring bicycles actually come equipped with a Dynamo hub pre-installed, so they are usually an aftermarket purchase, or are included at request with a custom-built bicycle.

Tires & Tubes

The tires of your bicycle are more important than you might think. After air drag, the tire is the second largest source of power consumption on your bike.

With the right tire, your bicycle will ride like a dream, providing you with the proper amount of suspension, while at the same time allowing you to pedal efficiently, balance properly and propel yourself through turns.

Pick the wrong tire, however, and you'll not only be expending a lot more energy as you pedal, but you'll be opening yourself up to countless problems, such as flat tires, lack of traction and even damage to your wheels and frame.

Tire Composition

There are a number of different bicycle tire types, but in most cases (99%) the type of tire on your bicycle is going to be a conventional bicycle tire called a "clincher" or sometimes a "wire-on." These types of tires consist of an outer tire with a U-shaped cross section and a separate inner tube. The edges of the tire hook over the edges of the wheel rim and air pressure from the inner tube holds everything in place.

Clincher tires, while they may appear to be made entirely of rubber when viewed from the outside, are actually comprised of three very important components: bead, fabric and rubber.

The bead is found at the very edge of the tire, where the tire makes contact with the rim of your bicycle's wheel. The bead is made up of several hoops of strong steel cable or Kevlar cord. It is this part of your tire that actually holds everything together.

The fabric is what forms the body of your bicycle tire. The fabric runs from the bead on one side of the tire to the bead on the other side and it is the shape of this fabric that ultimately determines the shape of your bicycle tire. Most manufacturers use some sort of nylon cord for the fabric of the tires, although cotton and canvas were commonly used in the past and Kevlar is sometimes used as a puncture preventative.

Finally, the rubber is the exterior part of the tire that we see from the outside when we ride a bicycle. The rubber is placed onto the tire's fabric so as to prevent the fabric from damage, but the rubber itself has no structural importance. The rubber that comes into contact with the ground, however, is called "tread" and this part of the tire's design may or may not play a part in how much traction your tire creates with the ground.

Traction

Traction is the word we use to describe a bicycle's ability to grip the road surface and prevent any kind of skidding or slipping. When you are in an upright position and riding your bicycle in a straight or relatively straight line, traction isn't much of a concern. But as soon as you brake, climb a steep hill or attempt to turn a corner, traction suddenly becomes very important.

When it comes to traction, there are five vital elements that play a part in whether you will stay upright or begin to slip and slide:

- ⅄ The inflation pressure of your tube/tire.

- ⅄ The type of rubber (or rubber formula) used in your specific brand of tires.

- ⅄ The tread pattern of your tires.

- ⅄ The suspension or lack thereof on your bicycle.

- ⅄ Your posture on the bike and general ability to ride with proper technique.

By adjusting these five elements, you either increase your traction with the road and therefore decrease your rolling-resistance (how easily your bicycle rolls over the ground) or you decrease the traction you have with the road and increase your rolling-resistance.

Width & Pressure

When it comes to putting air in your tires, you should remember that wider tires generally call for lower pressures and narrower tires call for higher pressures. No matter what type of tires you have on your touring bicycle, getting the right pressure in the tires is important, as pressure ultimately determines your traction and rolling-resistance with the road.

Under inflate your tires and you will have more rolling-resistance, be more prone to flat tires, may needlessly bounce up and down on the road surface and your tires may even come off the rims when you go around a corner.

Over inflate your tires, on the other hand, and your tires will be more prone to damage from sharp rocks and similar road hazards and you will experience a rough ride on anything but the smoothest of pavements.

Proper inflation, on the other hand, will provide you with negligible rolling- resistance, fewer flat tires, the ability to absorb minor road bumps and irregularities and the right amount of traction (which will prevent you from crashing, slipping or sliding).

The question now is, "What exactly is the right pressure for your tires?"

Well, most tires have a recommended pressure marked on the side of the tire by the manufacturer. This number is either the maximum pressure that the manufacturer recommends, or is a range of possible pressures, from low to high.

While people who are new to cycling tend to stick strictly to the recommended tire pressures that the manufacturers provide, more experienced cyclists tend to push their tire pressures to the limit by going outside of the recommended pressure settings and/or varying these pressures depending on the surface type they find themselves cycling on

Ultimately, the correct pressure for any given tire depends on the load that the tire is being asked to support. A heavier cyclist, for example, is going to need a higher tire pressure than a lighter cyclist might need.

On a similar note, when you want to travel off-road or into conditions where snow, dirt or mud play a regular part of the cycling experience, lower tire pressures are the way to go. However, lowering your pressure too much may result in pinch flats and/or your tire coming completely off the rim.

Tread Patterns

When it comes to tire tread, the tread is really only important when you are riding in off-road conditions. Contrary to popular belief, bicycle tires for on-road use have no need for tread of any kind. In other words, the best bicycle tires for on-road riding don't have any tread at all.

If the last paragraph caught you by surprise, you should know that the tread you see on some road and touring bike tires is a marketing gimmick in which tire manufacturers are able to increase their number of sales by selling treaded tires to inexperienced cyclists who believe that a good tire has to have tread on it.

In reality, narrow cycling tires deform as they come into contact with pavement (pavement that is usually deeper and rougher than the tread on the tires themselves). As the tires make contact with the pavement, they temporarily acquire the shape of the pavement texture, thereby creating traction with the road surface. Adding additional tread to a narrow bicycle tire is therefore extraneous and unnecessary.

The larger, deeper and knobbier tread found on mountain bike tires (and off- road touring bicycles), however, does help to increase your traction in two dis- tinct ways:

The knobs on the tread work to hook onto and push off of any hard, irregular surfaces on the ground.

On soft, squishy surfaces (such as dirt, mud and certain types of snow) the knobs on mountain bike tires dig into the ground and actually help your bike to grip the road surface.

Using knobby, treaded tires is great for off-road riding, or in conditions where there might be a thin later of ice or snow on the ground. When it comes to riding in these sorts of conditions, look for tires where the tread is widely spaced apart. This type of tread allows for large clusters of dirt, mud and snow to be pushed out and away from the tire, which will provide you with the most traction possible.

Most people assume, however, that in wet and rainy weather, tread is an absolute must. But the truth is, both knobby and treadless road tires respond in pretty much the same way in wet, slick conditions. They slip and slide! All tires do. Tread makes little to no improvement in these types of conditions.

Presta vs. Schrader Valves

There are two different types of bicycle valves used in the touring bike world - Presta valves and Schrader valves.

The Schrader valve (sometimes called the American valve) is a brand of pneumatic tire valve used on virtually every motor vehicle in the world.

A Schrader valve consists of an externally threaded hollow cylindrical metal tube, typically made of brass. In the center of the exterior end of the valve is a metal pin pointing along the axis of the tube, with the pin's end approximately flush with the end of the valve body. On top of the valve is a valve cap, which is important for preventing dirt and water from entering the outside of the valve. If dirt and water were to enter the valve, a jam or contamination could occur, resulting in a leak.

This type of valve is common not just on cars, trucks and motorcycles, but on many wide-rimmed bicycle wheels as well (most commonly seen in commuting and off-road touring bicycles).

Presta valves (sometimes called Sclaverand or French valves), on the other hand, are commonly found on road-styled touring bicycles.

A Presta valve is made up of an outer valve stem and an inner valve body with a lock nut attached to the base of the valve to secure the stem at the wheel rim and a valve cap at the other end.

The outer valve stem is manufactured in various lengths for different applications and has a narrower diameter (6 mm) than the Schrader valve (8 mm), which helps strengthen narrow rims because the weakest point of a bicycle rim is usually the valve hole.

A small screw and nut on the top of the valve body allows the valve to be screwed shut and ensure that it remains tightly closed. The nut must be unscrewed to permit airflow in either direction (this must be done before attaching a pump) and the screw remains captive on the valve body even when unscrewed fully. It is tightened again after the tire is inflated and the pump removed.

The valve cap on a Presta valve, like the valve cap of a Schrader valve, protects the valve body, but is not necessary to prevent pressure loss.

In general, you will see Presta valves on most touring bike models (especially Sport Touring, Light Touring and Road Touring bicycles), whereas Schrader valves are more common on Commuting and Off-Road Touring Bicycles.

While neither valve type is bad, the advantage to Schrader valves is that they can generally be found in any part of the world, whereas Presta valves may be difficult (or impossible) to find in undeveloped countries.

Gearing

Once you start looking at touring bicycles, you will begin to notice that there are a number of different gear combinations used on the various models. In fact, there are thousands of possible gear combinations, and all of them have benefits and drawbacks of some kind. There is no perfect gearing setup or gear combination.

While I recommend you leave the gearing choices to the experts (as most touring bicycles come equipped with more than enough gears for your needs (and the derailleurs you use on your bike will vary depending on the type of gearing you select), this chapter will introduce you to the basics of gear selection and give you some general tips for picking out a bicycle with the best gearing setup for the type of bicycle touring in which you plan to participate.

Every touring bicycle will have a different number of gears (with most touring bikes having between 24 and 27 total gear options). The gearing on true touring bicycles is very similar to the gearing found on many mountain bike models. There are a number of low gears (a small chainring in the front and larger sprockets in the back) to help you climb up steep hills and easily transport the extra weight you are going to be carrying on your bicycle, while at the same time providing you with some of the larger, faster gears needed for cycling quickly on flat paved roads.

A common way to look at the gearing on a touring bicycle is to list its crankset sizes as a series of numbers.

For example: 30/39/50

What these numbers tell you is that the bicycle in question has three chainrings. The smallest chainring (the one that will help you the most when climbing steep hills) has a total of 30 teeth on it. The middle chainring (the one you will use the most on flat ground) has 39 teeth. And the largest chainring (the one you use for going downhill or sprinting at high speeds) has a total of 50 teeth.

These numbers, however, do not take into account the gears on the rear cassette of your bicycle, which commonly have a teeth pattern that looks a little something like this: 12-13-14-15-16-17-19-21

While an entire book could be written about bicycle gearing systems, possible gear combinations and how all these various gears affect your performance on the bike, the most important numbers to look at on a touring bike are those two or three numbers that are listed next to the "crankset" of the bicycle.

The smallest number (in this case, 30) is the number that is of most concern when buying a touring bicycle, as this will be the lowest gear you can get into when climbing with your bike.

Most quality touring bike models come with a lowest crankset gear that has anywhere between 22 and 30 total teeth, with 26 teeth being the most popular on Road Touring models.

With speed being less of a concern for most touring cyclists, the middle and larger chain rings are of less importance. It is that small chain ring that matters most... and if you plan on climbing a lot of hills, I recommend you get the smallest chainring possible.

Groupsets & Components

A groupset is a collection of bicycle parts (or components), excluding your bicycle's frame, fork, stem, wheels, tires, handlebars and saddle.

A groupset typically consists of:

⅄ 2 shifters (left and right)

- 2 brake levers (left and right)

- 2 brakes (front and rear)

- 2 derailleurs (front and rear)

- 1 bottom bracket

- 1 crankset

- 1 chain

- 1 cogset, freewheel or cassette

While all of these components can be purchased individually, bicycle manufacturers tend to bundle these parts together and offer them as a package for inclusion on various bicycle models, with each groupset being targeted at a different budget and/or use.

The most common groupset types have been listed below. Each manufacturer's groupset offering is arranged in descending order according to its price/quality.

Shimano Road Bicycles

- Dura-Ace 7900

- Ultegra 6700

- 105 5700

- Tiagra

- Sora

- 2300

Shimano Mountain Bicycles (commonly used on touring bicycles)

- XTR

- Saint
- Deore XT
- Hone
- SLX
- Deore LX
- Deore
- Alivio
- Acera
- Altus
- Tourney

Campagnolo Road Bicycles

- Super Record
- Record
- Chorus
- Athena
- Centaur
- Veloce

SRAM Road Bicycles

- Red
- Force
- Rival

- Apex

SRAM Mountain Bicycles

- XX

- X0

- X9

- X7

- X5

- X4

- X3

The cost of your touring bicycle is going to depend not only on the type of metal used in the frame of the bike itself, but also on the type and quality of components used on that bicycle. Components play a large part in determining the price of your bicycle.

Therefore, while I generally recommend you get the best possible components you can afford, the best components are going to be out of reach for many people looking to purchase a touring bicycle. That said, you shouldn't be afraid of buying a bicycle just because it comes with a groupset that isn't at the top of the lists above. Compare prices across various touring bike models and get the bicycle with the best components you can afford.

Brake Types

The brakes on your bicycle are used to slow you down and bring you to a stop. Because of the extra loads that are carried on touring bicycles, it is important that you have a good, working set of brakes.

There are two main types of brakes used on touring bicycles today: rim brakes and disc brakes.

Rim Brakes

Rim brakes get their name because the braking force is applied by friction pads to the rim of the rotating wheel, thus slowing it and the bicycle to an eventual stop. The brake pads on rim brakes are either made of leather or rubber and are mounted in metal "shoes." Rim brakes are typically activated by squeezing a lever mounted on your handlebar.

However, rim brakes perform poorly when the rims are wet and they require regular maintenance. Brake pads wear down and have to be replaced. Over the long run, rims also become worn. Therefore, rims should be checked for wear periodically as they can fail catastrophically if the braking surface becomes too worn.

Rim brakes also heat up the rim every time you use them. In normal use this isn't a problem, as the brakes are applied with limited force and only for a short period of time. However, on a fully-loaded bicycle or on a long descent, the heat generated by rim brakes can increase the temperature so much that the tube can increase the tire pressure and blow the tire completely off the wheel. If this happens on the front wheel, a serious accident is almost inevitable. This is quite rare, but caution should be taken to make sure your rims do not overheat when using this particular type of braking mechanism.

In the end, rim brakes are a good option for the traveling cyclist because they are cheap, light, mechanically simple, easy to maintain, easy to find replacement parts for almost anywhere in the world and relatively powerful.

Disc Brakes

A disc brake consists of a metal disc attached to the wheel hub that rotates with the wheel. Calipers are attached to the frame or fork along with pads that squeeze together on the disc. As the pads drag against the disc, the bicycle is slowed.

In basic operation, disc brakes are practically identical to rim brakes, but disc brakes typically provide a much stronger stopping capability. Disc brakes are the same type of brakes used on many motorcycles and automobiles because they are effective at stopping heavy, fast-moving vehicles in a short distance.

While disc brakes are great for touring bicycles because they are so good at stopping a fast and heavy bicycle in a short amount of time, the main disadvantage is that for someone who is planning to travel around the world (and into areas where bike shops are few and far between), finding spare parts could become a problem.

This becomes even more of a problem if you opt for hydraulic disc brakes. When looking at disc brakes on touring bicycles, you will encounter two main types: cable and hydraulic. While cable brakes are considered inferior to hydraulic disc brakes, they are easier to fix and realign. Hydraulic brakes are considered the best, but are harder to adjust and repair when on the road, as they require a number of special tools to work on.

Using disc brakes may also require that you purchase special racks and/or panniers for your touring bicycle, so be sure to do your research before purchasing a touring bicycle with disc brakes. While disc brakes are popular on many modern bikes (and are becoming increasingly more popular on touring bicycles), they are not always the best choice (especially if you are planning a bicycle tour in a remote corner of the world).

Handlebars

There are three common types of handlebars found on most touring bike models. Your handlebars are not only the tool you use to steer your bicycle, but they also function as one of three surfaces on which to support your body weight as you ride (the other two being your saddle and your pedals), in addition to being a convenient mounting place for your bicycle's shifters, brake levers, lights, bell, cycling computer, GPS or other optional accessories.

Drop Handlebars

Drop handlebars are common on both road and touring bike models. They are flat at the top, near the stem, and then make either a shallow or steep drop downward toward the sides. These types of handlebars are common in the touring world because they provide you with a number of different positions in which to place your hands as you ride, which is important when spending long hours on the bike each day.

Drop handlebars are more common on American touring bicycles than they are on European touring bike models.

Flat Handlebars

Flat or "riser" bars are the standard handlebars equipped on most mountain bicycles and hybrids. They can also be found on many touring bike models. A flat handlebar is a nearly-straight tube, slightly bent toward the rider.

Flat bars are more common on European touring bicycles than they are on American touring bike models.

Butterfly Handlebars

Sometimes referred to as "touring" or "trekking" bars, these types of handlebars are commonly encountered in continental Europe, although they can be found on American touring bikes as well.

Butterfly handlebars typically consist of a broken figure-eight arrangement mounted horizontally on the stem. This style of bar allows the rider to remain relatively upright (unlike drop handlebars) while at the same time providing a wide range of hand positions to keep you comfortable on long rides.

The type of handlebar you ultimately select is going to depend on two major factors:

⊿   The type of handlebars available in your region of the world.

⊿   Personal preference.

Riding bicycles with each of these three handlebar setups before purchasing your ideal touring bike will enable you to determine which type of handlebar setup you prefer the most.

Shifters

The type of handlebars you have on your bicycle will determine which type of shifters you can use. This chapter will give you a breakdown of the four basic types of touring bike shifters.

If you opt for drop handlebars, you will have two basic types of shifters to choose from: bar-end shifters and brake-shift combo shifters.

Bar-End Shifters

Bar-end shifters are simple, robust shifters that are fitted into the very end of drop handlebars, where the handlebar plug would normally be. These types of shifters were originally designed for racing, as the rider would want to be able to shift gears while in an aerodynamic tucked position. Over the years, however, bar-end shifters have become popular on touring bicycles due to the fact that they are inexpensive and easier to repair than many other types of bicycle shifters.

Brake-Shift Combo Shifters

This type of shifter puts both the brake and shifter controls literally at your fingertips. Brake-shift combo shifters (also called "integrated shifters" or just plain "shifters" combine what would normally be two separate parts (the brake levers and the shifters) into one easy to control and aerodynamic device, and are located at the very front of your bicycle, on both the far left and far right sides of the handlebars.

If drop handlebars are not your style, however, and you decide to use a touring bicycle with either flat or butterfly handlebars, you will usually be limited to either one or two of the following types of shifters: thumb shifters and/or grip shifters.

Thumb Shifters

Popular on mountain bikes, hybrids and a number of other bicycle models, thumb shifters are mounted either to the top or bottom of flat handlebars and with the push of your thumb, allow you to either shift up a gear or shift down (depending on which way you push the shifters). Thumb shifters are easy to install, repair and use.

Grip Shifters

Grip shifters (also called "twist shifters") are integrated into the design of some flat handlebars, which allows you to change gears by simply twisting the grips forward or backward as you ride. Popular on inexpensive bicycles, grip shifters are usually only seen in the touring world on some folding bike models, as grip shifters, due to their integrated design, take up less space on the handlebars when compared with thumb shifters.

Seats / Saddles

Most (but not all) touring bicycles come with a saddle (also called a "seat").

The few touring bikes that don't come with saddles are typically those that are custom ordered and/or custom built, as the manufacturer of these types of bicycles probably figures that if you are selective enough to be ordering a custom bicycle, you'll probably want a custom saddle to go along with it.

In most cases, you don't need to order a new or custom saddle for your touring bike, and the saddle that comes with the touring bicycle you buy will work out just fine in 90% of the cases.

However, almost anyone that rides a bicycle for an extended period of time (like you tend to do while bicycle touring) will experience some kind of butt or crotch pain as they ride. It is during these moments that many cyclists wonder if they need to get a better saddle for their bike.

The truth is, if you are experiencing butt or crotch pain as you ride, your saddle is probably not the problem.

The pain you are experiencing as you ride is usually either caused by ill-fitting clothes, excess body fat (which then rubs against your saddle in a painful sort of way), or an improper adjustment of your bicycle's saddle, seat post or handlebars.

There is no one bicycle saddle that will magically alleviate your butt or crotch pain as you ride. Every person is different, with a different body type and dimensions, and this means that the saddle that works well for one person might not work so wonderfully for the next.

In general, however, you want a bicycle saddle that is firm, but also has a small amount of give to it. You don't want a bicycle saddle that is as hard as a rock and you don't want one of those super cushy gel-type saddles either (because soft saddles usually make your butt chaff).

Shopping for a saddle is just like shopping for a mattress. You want something that is firm at its core, but soft at its surface. If your saddle fits those specifications and you are still experiencing pain as you ride, the problem is likely due the position of your saddle, seat post or handlebars (and not the saddle itself).

If your butt or crotch is hurting you while you ride your bike, try the following before going out and purchasing a new saddle:

- ⅄ Adjust the up and down angle of your saddle.

- ⅄ Adjust the side to side angle of your saddle.

- ⅄ Adjust the height of your seat post.

- Adjust the height of your handlebars.

- Adjust the position of your handlebars so you don't have to lean too far forward or too far back.

- Try sitting further up or further back on the saddle.

Remember that your saddle should be relatively level. If it is angled more than a few degrees up or down, there is probably something wrong.

Also, remember that the full weight of your body is not meant to rest entirely on your saddle. Resting your full body-weight on your bicycle's seat is obviously going to cause you some pain. Instead, your saddle is just one of three areas on which you should be spreading out the weight of your body. As you ride, your weight should be dispersed between your butt/crotch and your saddle, your hands and your handlebars and your pedals and your feet.

Finally, once you find a position for your saddle that you like, don't move it! You might even want to put a little electrical tape around the seatpost (just above the seatpost clamp) so that if you have to remove the seatpost for any reason, you will be able to quickly and easily get your saddle back in its proper position.

Pedals & Shoes

The pedal is the part of a bicycle that you push with your feet in order to propel your bike forward. The pedal provides the connection with your bike between your foot and shoe, and is therefore one of the most important parts of your bicycle.

While there are a number of different pedal types available, there are really only two types of pedals that are popular in the touring bike world: SPD and platform.

SPD Pedals

SPD pedals, which stands for "Shimano Pedaling Dynamics," are a type of clipless pedal (also referred to as "clip-in" or "step-in" pedal) that are used in conjunction with a special cycling shoe with a metal cleat fitted to the sole, which locks into a mechanism in the pedal and thus holds the shoe firmly to the pedal. The design of the clipless pedal allows you to twist your shoe in such a way that you can both lock and unlock your feet from the pedals, while at the same time having the rotational float needed to prevent injury to your joints as you ride.

The advantage to this type of pedal/shoe system is that it provides you with the most efficient means of pedaling your bicycle. With your foot locked to the pedal as you ride, you can not only increase your power on the downstroke, but harness additional power on the upstroke as well.

In addition to making your time on the bicycle more efficient, SPD pedals also allow you to walk short distances in relative comfort. While you wouldn't want to wear an SPD cycling shoe to hike a distance of 1 mile/1 kilometer or more, you can use the shoe to comfortably cover short distances on foot (which is especially important for touring cyclists like yourself).

Platform Pedals

The other type of pedal you might consider is the basic platform pedal (also called "flat pedals"). This is the type of pedal that comes standard with many bicycle models (not just touring bikes) and can be used with just about any type of shoe.

This type of pedal is inexpensive and made of either plastic and/or metal. It consists of a large, flat area on which to rest your feet as you pedal and can be used with non-cycling specific shoes.

Unlike SPD pedals, however, which allow you to power your bike on both the downstroke and the upstroke, platform pedals only allow you to power your bike while pressing down and are therefore less efficient than SPD pedal systems.

This can be changed, however, by simply adding a set of toe clips or toe straps to your platform pedals. Toe clips are a small plastic or metal cage that extend out of your platform pedals and reach up over the tops of your toes. Toe straps are very much like toe clips, but consist of a basic fabric or leather strap that slides over the top of your foot, rather than wrap all the way around it like a cage.

Both toe clips and toe straps, however, function in much the same way. By wrapping over the top part of your foot/toes, they allow you to transfer power from your legs to your bike on both the downstroke and the upstroke (in much the same way that SPD pedal systems allow you to do).

While many touring bicycles come equipped with either platform pedals or platform pedals and a set of toe clips, many touring bike models come with no pedals at all. This is because touring bike manufacturers know that the type of pedal you select is a personal choice and differs from person to person. Just know that you if you order a bicycle that does not come equipped with a set of pedals, this is an extra expenses that you will need to add to the total cost of your bike.

Extras You May Need To Purchase

Speaking of things you might need to add to your bicycle once you purchase it, now would be a good time to talk about some of the extra parts, items and accessories you may need to purchase for your touring bicycle before you are ready to hit the road on your first big bicycle tour.

Pedals

Many touring bicycles come equipped with inexpensive platform pedals. But most touring bikes don't come with pedals of any type. Depending on the type of bicycle tour you wish to participate in, you will likely need to purchase a set of appropriate pedals before you can take your new bike out for a spin.

Racks

A luggage carrier, also commonly called a rack, is a device on a bicycle to which cargo or panniers can be attached. Racks are popular features on both utility and touring bicycles. Racks may be mounted on the front or rear of a bicycle, although the rear mount is more common.

Many, but not all touring bicycles come with either one or two racks. Some of the more inexpensive touring bike models may come with a rack, but the rack is so flimsy that it needs to be replaced before any real touring can be done.

The front and rear racks are typically, but not always, an extra purchase that you need to make.

Panniers

A pannier is a basket, bag, box or similar container, carried in pairs and slung over the rack of a bicycle. There are many styles of bicycle panniers. Touring panniers come in both rear and front styles, usually sold in pairs, intended to hold enough equipment for self-sustained tours over several days or weeks.

Commuters who bicycle have pannier options designed to hold laptop computers, files and folders, changes of clothes or shoes and lunches. Some cyclists create makeshift pannier bags out of grocery bags, grocery baskets, garment-bags, convertible backpacks and various multi-purpose bags as alternatives to purchasing a commercial pannier.

Panniers, like many touring bicycles, are made and sold in various countries all around the world. While one type of bicycle touring pannier may be popular in America, for example, it may be almost impossible to find in other parts of the world. Therefore, your option of bicycle panniers may be limited to the types of panniers available in your part of the world.

Trailer

Trailers can be used with touring bicycles or just about any type of bicycle on the market. If you want to take short trips with your bicycle, but don't want to invest in a specially-built touring bicycle, hauling your gear in a trailer is a great way to go! While most bicycle touring trailers aren't cheap, they are certainly less expensive than buying a new touring-specific bicycle.

Trailers are popular for long-distance touring cyclists as well—even those who have touring-specific bikes. In some scenarios (especially off-road riding), trailers typically outperform rack and pannier systems and are therefore popular amongst touring cyclists who travel on dirt roads, single-track trails and remote, uncivilized locations.

Fenders or Mudguards

Fenders are a part that attaches to your bicycle that wraps itself around and frames the wheels. Their primary purpose is to prevent sand, mud, rocks, liquids, and other road spray from being thrown into the air by the rotating tire. Bicycle fenders are typically made of either metal or plastic and can be damaged by contact with the road surface.

A mudguard is another term used to describe bicycle fenders.

A mud flap, on the other hand, is used in combination with fenders or mudguards to protect bicycle riders, other vehicles and pedestrians from mud and other flying debris thrown into the air by a bicycle's rotating tire. A mud flap is typically made from a soft flexible material such as rubber that is not easily damaged by contact with flying debris, the tire or the road surface.

Some touring bicycles come with fenders, but most do not. While fenders/mudguards are not 100% necessary, they are a nice thing to have if you plan on cycling in wet, rainy conditions on a regular basis and you should consider the extra cost of fenders before purchasing a new touring bicycle.

Water Bottles & Cages

A bottle cage is a metal or plastic device used to affix a water bottle to a bicycle. Composed of plastic, aluminum, stainless steel, titanium or carbon fiber, cages are most often times attached to the frame of a bicycle. Most modern bicycles have threaded holes in the frame to hold the bottle cage, often times called braze-ons, even though they may be welded, glued, riveted or molded into the frame material. Most bicycles are equipped to carry two water bottle cages, although many touring bicycles come with mounts for three or more bottle cages.

Lights

While front and rear lights are not always necessary, they are required by law in several parts of the world. Even if you don't plan to ride your bike at night, equipping your bicycle with both a front and rear light is a good idea.

When purchasing a set of lights, remember that there are two basic kinds: lights that help others see you... and lights that help you see where you are going.

Not all bicycle lights are meant to help you see in dark, nighttime conditions. If you want to see where you are going, you will typically need to spend a lot more money on a lighting setup than someone who simply wants to make sure that the people and vehicles in the immediate area can see him or her.

Bell

Another non-necessity for the most part, the bicycle bell is a nice little thing to have in crowded urban environments where you may find yourself either cycling amongst or walking your bike through a crowd of people and/or other cyclists. In many European countries, for example, it is considered both polite and proper to ring your bell before passing another cyclist on a bike path or in the street. In fact, some countries in the world require that you have a bell of some kind on your bike.

Other Cycling & Bicycle Touring Essentials

In addition to all this, you are going to want to equip yourself with all the other basics that are needed when riding a bicycle.

This includes items such as a:

- ⋏ Multi-Tool

- ⋏ Bike Pump

- ⋏ Spoke Wrench

- ⋏ Spare Tube(s)

- ⋏ Tire Levels

- ⋏ And more!

For a complete list of bicycle touring essentials (including a breakdown of the clothing, camping equipment, electronics, and other items) needed for long distance bicycle touring, please see:

www.bicycletouringbook.com

How To Purchase A New Touring Bicycle

You would think that in this modern day and age, you would be able to simply log onto your computer and pick out the ideal touring bicycle and have it delivered to your home a few days later. That may be the case in the very near future, but at the moment the process of ordering a touring bicycle is very much the same as it has been for the past fifty years or more—you're going to need to go to your local bike shop and place an order.

The problem is, touring bikes are a rare breed in the bicycle world and few bike shops carry touring bicycles of any kind. This makes test driving a bike before you buy it both difficult and occasionally impossible.

While there are a few touring bicycles that can be ordered online, and a few large retailers may carry a touring bike or two at their local stores, most touring bicycles have to be special ordered from dealers at your local bike shop.

Once you find a bicycle you are interested in and want to either find out more about or actually purchase, the next step is to locate a dealer of that particular kind of bicycle in your area. You can usually find a list of local dealers by performing a quick internet search or by visiting the bicycle manufacturer's website and searching their online database for dealers in your area.

You may find that with some touring bicycles, there are no dealers in your area. In some cases, there may not even be a dealer in your country! And in more extreme (but not totally unfamiliar cases) you may not have a single dealer on your entire continent.

The trick, however, is to a find a dealer (whether local or half way around the world) and call them on the phone (or send them an email). Once you have made contact with the dealer, you need to tell them what kind of bicycle you want, what size bike you need, and any other options and/or upgrades you might want to order with the bicycle.

The bike shop (if they are local) may have you come in at this time for a fitting, just to make sure you get the right size bicycle. Or the shop may send you a form that you can use to measure yourself, jot down your dimensions and mail, fax or email the form back to the bike shop. This form will help to ensure that the bicycle being ordered for you is actually the right size.

After you have sent in your measurements and placed your order, the bike shop will place an order with the manufacturer and it may take anywhere from one week to one month or more for your bicycle to be shipped from the manufacturer to your local dealer.

Once the bicycle arrives at the shop, the dealer will assemble the bicycle for you and give you a call once the bike is ready to be picked up.

In the event that you are ordering your bicycle from overseas, you may make a request with the dealer you are working with that the bicycle be shipped to your home address. Some dealers will be happy to do this for you, as long as you understand that the bicycle may need some assembling once it arrives (which you can either do yourself or you can take it to a local bike shop to have it assembled for you) and other dealers will be hesitant to mail the bicycle at all (usually because they are fearful that with the bike arriving in pieces, you will be unhappy with the bike upon arrival and want to return it).

While ordering through a dealer is the typical approach to buying a new touring bicycle, there are times when you may need to order the bicycle straight from the manufacturer. In these instances, the process is very similar.

The manufacturer will ask what bicycle, size, and options you want. Then they will explain how the bike is to be delivered. Sometimes you will need to go and pick up the bike yourself. Other times the bike will be delivered to your home address or a local bike shop in your area.

The Best Time Of Year To Purchase A Touring Bicycle

Touring bicycles can be purchased at any time of year, but the most popular time to buy a touring bicycle is in the spring when everyone seems to be gearing up for their summer bicycle touring adventures.

However, because touring bikes are such a rare breed of bicycle, and because everyone seems to buy their touring bikes at the same time, spring can be a somewhat hectic time to purchase a new touring bicycle.

Some of the companies that produce touring bicycles are quite small, and when spring rolls around, they can get a lot of orders all at once. Lacking the man and machine power necessary to quickly deliver the bicycles that have been ordered, some of these small companies can get quite backed up, causing long delivery delays that may affect your ability to ride your new touring bicycle as soon as you had hoped.

My recommendation for avoiding this scenario, of course, is to buy your new touring bicycle well in advance of any travels that you may wish to do with it. Not only do you need a fair amount of time to get used to riding your new bicycle before using it on tour, but you need to factor in the amount of time needed for a small (and even large) bicycle manufacturer to process all the new orders they have received. Ordering your new touring bicycle three or more months in advance is highly recommended.

Avoiding the crowds of spring cycling is one thing, but if you're looking to save a lot of money on the purchase of your new touring bike, you may want to buy your bicycle in the fall.

With the new year quickly approaching, bicycle dealers and manufactures alike need to get rid of their current models and make way for the new bicycle models that will be arriving in just a couple months. So, what do they do? They sell the bicycles they still have in stock at a discount!

If you are lucky enough to find a touring bicycle for sale between the months of September and December (if you are in the Northern Hemisphere), it is not uncommon to save hundreds of dollars off the normal retail price of that bicycle. For bargain hunters and the financially strained, autumn is the best time to shop for a new or used touring bicycle.

Buying A Used Touring Bicycle

You can search online for used touring bicycles, but they are rare and difficult to find. If you are able to snatch up a quality touring bike on

Ebay.com or Craigslist.org, consider yourself lucky.

More commonly, used touring bicycles are sold at garage sales and within several of the touring bike communities that exist online.

Check, for example:

- Local Bike Trader

- Crazy Guy On A Bike

Even on some manufacturer's websites you will find listings for used touring bicycles.

When looking at used bicycles, be sure to ask about any crashes that may have occurred with the bike. If the bike has been crashed, look for cracks of breaks in the frame and other components.

Note the bicycle's tires, chain, cables and other parts. Excessive rust, cracking or wear should act as a warning.

Some things area easily repaired or replaced (such as handlebar tape or bent water bottles cages), but other problem areas (such as a noisy bottom-bracket or a faulty rear cassette) can set you back hundreds of dollars.

Do You Need A Custom Touring Bicycle?

In most cases, no, you don't need a custom-built touring bicycle. But going custom is a perfectly acceptable option, so long as you are willing and able to spend the extra money needed to acquire a custom-built bike.

Most standard bicycle sizes are fine for the majority of touring bike buyers. The people who go custom, on the other hand, tend to do so for one of three reasons.

A touring bike customer orders a custom bicycle because they either have a physical abnormality that makes going custom the only way to go (it could be their height, weight or a physical condition that causes them pain when they ride a normal bicycle).

Other times, people order custom-built bicycles because they are embarking on an adventure that is truly unique and they either need or want a bicycle that is uniquely suited for their upcoming travels.

More commonly, however, people order custom-built bicycles simply because they want to—not because they necessarily need to.

While there is nothing wrong with going custom, many people needlessly convince themselves they need a custom-built bike for one of the two legitimate reasons above.

While ordering a custom built bicycle is fine, and can even be a lot of fun (especially for people who like to get overly detailed about the bicycles they ride, the components they use and the accessories they have), most people will not need to go the custom-built route.

For most individuals, searching for a preassembled touring bicycle like the ones listed inside this book will be the easiest, fastest, most affordable and best overall route to take.

Touring Bike Scams You Should Know About

In your search for the perfect touring bicycle, you may encounter the bicycle salesman who tries to push a bicycle on you that isn't really built for the type of bicycle touring you wish to participate in. This is why it is so important that you understand the different types of bicycle touring and have a basic understanding of the five major types of touring bicycles before you go out and search for a new touring bike at your local bike shops.

At some local dealers you will encounter a salesman who doesn't have the touring bike you both want and/or need, but he does have another kind of bicycle that he says "will work" and he wants to sell you that bike instead.

The dealer isn't necessarily trying to rip you off, but he probably doesn't have your best interest at heart. In some cases, the salesman may simply be uneducated about proper touring bicycles. The important thing to remember, however, is that the bicycle he is trying to sell you is probably not the one you should buy.

While some locals dealers will be super knowledgeable about touring bicycles and the various types of bicycle tours, other dealers wouldn't know a touring bicycle from a road, hybrid or mountain bike model if their life depended on it.

The secret to finding a good touring bicycle is to first of all know what kind of bicycle you need, and secondly, to search out a knowledgeable dealer who can help you find that bicycle in your size and with the additional options and add-ons that you desire.

Don't let a local dealer or online salesman push you into purchasing the wrong bicycle! This happens much more frequently than you might think.

Words You Should Know

As you begin your search for the perfect touring bicycle, you may begin to see the same words being used over and over again. In the event that you do not know what these words mean, here are their definitions:

Braze-Ons

A braze-on is the name for any number of parts of a bicycle which have been permanently attached to the frame. The term "braze-on" comes from when these parts would have been brazed onto steel frame bicycles.

Braze-ons continue to be so called even though they may be welded, glued, riveted or molded into the frame material, depending on the material itself and the connection method used elsewhere on the frame.

Braze-ons are usually used to describe the points on the bicycle where the fenders, racks and/or water bottle cages are attached by means of a small screw or bolt.

Butted Steel

Bicycle frames built using steel tubes that have been thinned out in the middle and thickened at the ends are referred to as "butted frames." Butted frames are designed this way so that they add strength where the frame needs it most (at the welds), while reducing the overall weight of the finished bicycle.

Cro-Moly

Cro-Moly (also referred to as CroMo, Cro-Mo, CroMoly, CrMo and a number of similar terms) is a type of steel that has been alloyed with chromium and molybendenum and is used in the production of touring bicycle frames. The addition of these two metals makes Cro-Moly steel lighter and stronger than regular steel. This allows touring bike manufacturers to use thinner frame tubes and reduce weight, while preserving the overall quality of the bicycle. Cro-Moly is one of the more expensive types of steel frame materials and is a popular material used in the production of touring bicycle frames.

Folding Bicycle

A folding bicycle is a bicycle designed to fold into a compact form, facilitating transport and storage. When folded, these types of bikes can be more easily carried into buildings and workplaces or onto public transportation—or more easily stored in compact living quarters or aboard a car, boat, train or plane. Folding mechanisms vary, with each offering a combination of folding speeds, folding ease, compactness, ride, weight, durability and price.

High-Tensile Steel

High-tensile steel (or "high-ten," as it is sometimes called) is a type of steel used in the production of low-end touring bicycle frames. Unlike Cro-Moly steel, high-tensile steel tubing contains few additional alloys, which help to make the steel both stronger and lighter. This means that high-tensile steel tends to be the heaviest and cheapest type of steel used in the production of touring bicycle frames.

Lugs

Lugs are sockets in the frame of your bicycle that the adjoining metal tubes slide into. Lugs provide additional support and stability, when compared to welded bicycle frames, but because of the extra materials that are used, they add weight to the finished bicycle.

Recumbent Bicycle

A recumbent bicycle is a bicycle that places the rider in a laid-back reclining position. Most recumbent riders choose this type of design for ergonomic reasons. Recumbent bicycles are available in a wide range of configurations, including: long to short wheelbase; large, small, or a mix of wheel sizes; overseat, underseat, or no-hands steering; and rear wheel or front wheel drive. Many of the people who ride recumbent bicycles do so because they suffer from back, neck or knee pain that prevents them from riding a traditional diamond-framed bicycle

S&S Couplers

An S&S coupler is a precision lug that is installed in a bicycle frame when it is manufactured to allow it to separate and pack for easy transportation. Full size road, touring or mountain bikes fitted with S&S couplers will often times fit inside a single 26" x 26" x 10" case that travels as regular airline luggage.

Tandem

The tandem bicycle is a form of bicycle designed to be ridden by more than one person. The term tandem refers to the seating arrangement (fore to aft, not side-by-side), not the number of riders. A bike with two riders side-by-side is called a "sociable." Bicycles for three, four or five riders are referred to as "triples" or "triplets", "quads" or "quadruplets" and "quints" or "quintuplets" respectively.

Tricycle or Trike

A tricycle (or trike) is a three-wheeled bicycle. While tricycles are often associated with the small three-wheeled vehicles used by pre-school aged children, they are also used by adults for a variety of purposes—including long-distance bicycle touring.

Summary Of Important Points

While touring bicycles may sometimes look a lot like the road, hybrid or mountain bike models you are familiar with, there are a number of minute details that make touring bicycles better designed for long-distance cycling and the transportation of heavy loads. For example:

- A frame design that favors comfort, stability and utility over speed.

- A long wheelbase (which makes the bicycle more comfortable and prevents the heels of your feet from hitting the panniers carried on your rear rack).

- Heavy duty forks and wheels (to help support the extra loads that touring bikes need to carry).

- Additional wheel spokes.

- Multiple mounting points (for front and rear racks, water bottle cages and fenders or mudguards).

- The ability to carry either two or four panniers mounted on front and/or rear racks.

⅄ Use standard parts and metals that are easy to repair and find replacement parts for (which is especially important if you plan to go bicycle touring in a remote part of the world where bicycle parts are either sparse or impossible to find).

⅄ Have handlebars that allow for multiple hand positions (which help to prevent injuries on long bicycle tours).

⅄ Have saddles that are more comfortable than those found on road or mountain bike models.

⅄ And come with a wide range of gears (especially low gears) so as to help you climb steep terrain while carrying a heavy load.

There are a number of different types of touring bicycles. Each type of touring bike has been designed for a different type of bicycle touring.

The secret to finding your ideal touring bicycle is to first determine which type of bicycle touring you want to conduct. Then you simply need to find a touring bicycle for that type of bicycle tour that is within your price range and is available in your region of the world.

There are three main types of bicycle tours (guided, self-guided and self-supported) with a number of different sub-types (day touring, overnight touring (or S24O), credit card touring, audax, randonneuring, light touring, ultralite touring, supported touring, guided self-supported touring, bikepacking, cyclocamping, expedition touring, loaded or fully-loaded touring, traditional bicycle touring, and bicycle travel).

There are five main types of touring bicycles. Each has been designed for a specific type of bicycle touring:

⅄ **Commuting** – Touring bicycles of this type are designed for short trips near your home. They make excellent commuter bicycles and can be used for short overnight and multi-day bike tours.

⅄ **Sport Touring** – Sport touring bicycles are designed to go fast and carry light loads. Perfect for credit-card touring, audax and randonneuring.

🔺 **Light Touring** – Comfortable bicycles than have been designed to carry light loads. Most of these bicycles can be equipped for lightweight bicycle tours, but lack some of the features found on full-fledged touring bicycles.

🔺 **Road Touring** – Designed for long-distance bicycle touring on paved roads and bicycle paths. Road touring bicycles can be mounted with front and rear racks and panniers and can typically handle a fair amount off-road riding.

🔺 **Off-Road Touring** – Designed to go anywhere and do just about anything. Off-road touring bicycles are built to be ridden where other touring bikes would struggle to go. Perfect for round-the-world bicycle touring.

You don't necessarily need a touring-specific bicycle in order to conduct a bicycle tour.

Determining whether or not you need a touring-specific bicycle depends on:

🔺 What kind of bicycle tour you wish to participate in.

🔺 How long you plan to be on the road.

🔺 What kind of bike you currently have.

🔺 What kind of condition your current bicycle is in.

🔺 Where in the world you plan to travel with your bicycle in the future.

🔺 What the road conditions are going to be like on your travels.

🔺 How much gear you plan to carry.

🔺 How comfortable you wish to be on your bike as you are

riding.

⅄ The amount of money you are willing to spend.

⅄ And a whole host of other factors.

If you are planning a short bicycle tour (less than a week in length), you can probably use the bicycle you already own. If your bicycle tour is more than a week in length, however, it is recommended that you look into purchasing a touring specific bicycle for your tour.

If you don't want to buy a touring-specific bicycle, you can always mount a trailer to the bicycle that you currently own.

If you choose to use a non-touring specific bicycle on a bicycle tour that is more than just a few days long, don't be surprised if you suffer from pain in your fingers, hands, arms, shoulders, neck, back, butt or crotch. Most road, hybrid and mountain bike models are not meant to be ridden for days on end.

Hard-tail mountain bikes are a good option for bicycle touring in many parts of the world (South America, Africa, parts of Asia, etc). Mountain bikes with front or rear suspension can be used with special racks made for suspension mountain bikes.

Steel (also referred to as CroMo or Cromoly) is the most common metal used in the production of touring bicycles frames and forks because steel is strong, flexible, and easy to repair just about anywhere in the world.

Steel, Aluminum, Titanium and Platinum are the four most popular metals used in the production of touring bicycle frames and forks.

Riding a bicycle with an aluminum frame for days on end may cause your body some pain and soreness, as aluminum of more rigid than steel and doesn't absorb as many of the bumps in the road. Instead, the bumps in the road and transferred to your back, butt, neck, arms and hands.

Carbon fiber frames and forks should be avoided when conducting bicycle tours of almost any type (although they can be used quite successfully for sport touring). Under the heavy loads that are carried on most bicycle tours, carbon fiber tends to crack and break.

The frame is the most important part of any touring bicycles. The components (i.e. derailleurs, shifters, brakes, etc.) can be changed and upgraded over time, but a weak, heavy, or uncomfortably stuff frame will remain with you no matter what. This is why selecting the correct frame size and metal type is so important.

Touring bicycles have a unique geometry that allow for:

- A more stable ride while carrying heavy loads.

- More sensitive steering.

- A lower center of gravity.

- And a more comfortable, upright riding position.

Make sure you get the correct size bicycle frame by standing over the bicycle's top tube and ensuring that there is about 1-2 inches between the top tube and your crotch. If there is more than 2 inches of space, the bicycle is probably too small for you. If there is less than 1 inch of space or your crotch is hitting the top tube, then the bicycle is too large for you.

Many touring bicycle companies/dealers will measure you or give you a measurement form to fill out to ensure that you are ordering the correct size bicycle frame.

If you are unsure about what size bicycle frame you need, go to your local bike shop and have them assist you. Some bicycle shops have special measurement equipment. Others will simply stand you over (or have you test ride) a few different bicycles sizes to determine which size bike is best for you.

There are two main types of bicycle wheels/tires used on touring bicycles (700c and 26 inch) and two less commonly used wheels/tires (29 inch and 20 inch).

700c wheels/tires are best used for cycling on paved roads and bicycle paths in countries and continents where replacement parts are plentiful and easy to find (such as North America, Europe and parts of Oceania and Asia).

26 inch wheels/tires are best used on off-road of mix-terrain bicycle tours and in countries where 700c wheels/tires might be difficult or impossible to find (such as South America, Africa, Asia and parts of Oceania).

Your bicycle's wheel is made up of three basic parts: the hub, the spokes and the rim.

Some touring bicycles have (or can be ordered to have) special hubs that either conduct electrcity (dynamo hubs), which can then be used to charge small electronic devices (such as cell phones, GPS units and lights) or hubs that contain complete gear systems (Rohloff hubs), which eliminate the gearing from the outside of your bicycle and place it all inside your bicycle's rear wheel.

Rohloff and dynamo hubs do not come standard with most touring bicycles. These special types of hubs are typically and after-market purchase or something that is special ordered when placing an order with a high-end touring bike manufacturer.

Most bicycle tires are made up of three separate components: beat, fabric and rubber.

The five elements that determine how much traction you have with the road surface are:

- The inflation pressure of your tubes/tires.

- The type of rubber (or rubber formula) used in your specific brand of tires.

- The tread pattern of your tires.

- The suspension or lack thereof on your bicycle.

⊥ Your posture on the bike and your ability to ride with proper technique.

Most touring bicycle tires are thicker than road bicycle tires and thinner than mountain bike tires.

You will want to put more air into your tires when riding a heavily loaded touring bicycle than when riding a bicycle carrying no load.

Under-inflate your tires and you will be more prone to flat tires and could cause permanent damage to the tires near where they attach to the rims.

Over-inflating your tires could cause a tire blow out, create a bumpy, painful bike riding experience and/or decreases your traction with the road surface.

Contrary to popular belief, the narrow road tires found on many touring bike models have no need for tread of any kind. The best bicycle tires for on-road riding don't have any tread at all.

If you are riding in off-road situations (or in parts of the world where snow and ice are common), choose a tire where the tread is widely spaced apart, as this type of tread allows for large clusters of dirt, mud and snow to pushed out and away from the tire, which will provide you with the most traction possible.

There are two main types of valves found on touring bicycle tubes: Presta and Schrader Valves.

Presta valve are usually found on Commuter or Off-Road touring bicycles and are easily found just about anywhere in the world.

Schrader valves are more commonly found on Sport Touring, Light Touring and Road Touring bicycles. Schrader valves are easily found in North America, Europe and parts of Oceania and Asia, but are extremely difficult to find in other parts of the world.

The gearing on a touring bicycle is typically displayed as a series of three numbers (For example: 30/39/50). These numbers refer to the bicycle's chainrings. The numbers tell you that this bicycle has three chainrings and that the smallest (and most important of the three chainrings) has 30 teeth on it.

Most touring bicycles have a small chainring with between 22 and 30 total teeth. 26 teeth if the most common size for the small chainring on most touring bicycles. If you plan to spend a lot of time climbing hills on your bicycle tours, and you want to have the easiest climb possible, look for a touring bicycle with the smallest chainring possible.

Like almost every other type of bicycle on the market, touring bicycles are usually fitted with a standard groupset of some kind. A groupset typically consists of:

- 2 shifters (left and right)

- 2 brake levers (left and right)

- 2 brakes (front and rear)

- 2 derailleurs (front and rear)

- 1 bottom bracket

- 1 crankset

- 1 chain

- 1 cogset, freewheel or cassette

The cost of your touring bicycle will vary greatly depending on the type and quality of the groupset that is used on the bike.

Many of the groupsets used on road or mountain bike models are also used on touring bicycles. A Sport Touring bicycle, for example, will probably have the same groupset found on a road racing bicycle. An Off-Road touring bicycle, however, might have the same groupset used on a mountain bike.

There are two main types of brakes found on touring bicycles: rim and disc brakes.

Rim brakes are preferred by traditional bicycle tourists because they are simple, inexpensive, easy to repair, and easy to find replacement parts for just about anywhere in the world.

Disc brakes are becoming more and more popular on modern touring bicycles because of their superior stopping power. However, disc brakes parts are difficult (and sometimes) impossible to find in many parts of the world. If you choose to use disc brakes on a round-the-world bicycle tour (or on a tour in a part of the world where you know it will be difficult to find replacement parts for your brakes), you may want to carry spare parts, just in case.

There are three types of handlebars commonly found on touring bicycles: drop handlebars, flat handlebars and butterfly handlebars.

While drop handlebars may look like the same type of handlebars seen on road racing bicycles, the purpose for the drops on a touring bicycle is not to decrease your wind drag, but to increase your total number of hand positions. The more you move you hands around while you ride, the less likely you are to suffer nerve damage.

Flat handlebars are usually found on European and/or Off-Road touring bicycles. They do not provide the multiple hand positions found with drop or butterfly handlebars.

Butterfly handlebars, like drop handlebars, give you multiple positions in which to place your hands as you ride, but also allow you to ride in a more comfortable upright riding position.

There are four main types of shifters found on most touring bicycles. If you opt for drop handlebars, you will have two basic types of shifters to choose from: bar-end shifters and brake-shift combo shifters. If drop handlebars are not your style, however, and you decide to use a touring bicycle with either flat or butterfly handlebars, you will usually be limited to either one or two of the following types of shifters: thumb shifters and/or grip shifters.

Some touring bicycles are sold without a seat/saddle.

Shopping for a quality bicycle touring saddle is just like shopping for a quality mattress. You want something that is firm at its core, but soft at its surface.

If your butt or crotch is hurting you while you ride your bike, try the following before going out and purchasing a new saddle:

- Adjust the up and down angle of your saddle.

- Adjust the side to side angle of your saddle.

- Adjust the height of your seat post.

- Adjust the height of your handlebars.

- Adjust the position of your handlebars so you don't have to lean too far forward or too far back.

- Try sitting further up or further back on the saddle.

The full weight of your body is not meant to rest entirely on your saddle. Instead, the weight of your body should be dispersed between your butt/crotch and your saddle, your hands and your handlebars and your feet and your pedals.

Once you find a comfortable position for your seat post and saddle, mark the location with a piece of take, a permanent market or a pencil so that if you need to move the saddle you can easily get it back into its ideal position.

When it comes to shoes and pedals, there are three main options: SPD pedals and shoes, regular tennis shoes with platform pedals, tennis shoes with platform pedals and toe clips.

Cycling with a pair of SPD pedals/shoes will give you the most powerful means of pedaling your bike, but SPD shoes are uncomfortable for walking distances more than 1 mile/kilometer.

Tennis shoes will be more comfortable to wear off the bike, and platform pedals are the least expensive pedal option, but tennis shoes and a flat platform pedal provide the least amount of power to your bicycle when you ride it.

If you want to be able to walk comfortably off the bike and still pedal your bicycle with some power (not just on the downstroke, but on the upstroke as well), you might choose to cycle in a pair of tennis shoes with platform pedal and a set of toe clips or straps.

Most touring bicycles do not come fully-equipped with everything you need to conduct a bicycle tour. In addition to purchasing a set of pedals and maybe even a saddle, you might also need to purchase a front and/or rear rack, front and/or rear panniers, a trailer, fenders or mudguards, lights, a bell, water bottles and water bottles cages, and a whole host of additional bicycle tools and equipment.

No touring bicycle is complete without at least the minimal maintenance and repair equipment.

- Multi-Tool
- Bike Pump
- Spoke Wrench
- Spare Tube(s)
- Tire Levels

Few touring bicycles can be purchased online. For most new bicycle purchases, you will need to first determine which type of bicycle you want to buy, then contact a local bicycle dealer in your area that carries that specific brand of bicycle. After deciding which bike you want to buy and double-checking to make sure you are ordering the correctly sized bicycle, your dealer will place an order with the manufacturer. The manufacturer will ship the bicycle to the dealer and the dealer will assemble the bicycle before contacting you to tell you that you new bicycle has arrived.

Most touring bicycle manufacturers will not ship a bicycle directly to your home. Even if you do find a manufacturer willing to ship you a bicycle, you will still need to assemble the bicycle once it arrives (or pay a local bike shop to assemble it for you).

If you can not find a local dealer in your area, you may have to deal with a dealer in a foreign state or country. Additional shipping, customs, taxes and assembly charges may apply for long-distance and/or international orders.

The best time to buy a touring bicycle (especially if you want to get a good price) is in the fall. It is at this time of year when most people are putting away their bicycles and bike shops are getting rid of their inventory, that you have the best chance of buying a brand new bicycle for (sometimes even) hundreds of dollars off its normal retail price.

You should purchase your touring bicycle at least three or more months in advance of the start of your bicycle tour. This will leave time not only for the bicycle to be made, delivered, and assembled, but also for you to test out, fully equip and get used to the bike before your bicycle tour begins.

Finding a used touring bicycle online or at your local bike shop is rare, but not impossible. Many people will buy a brand new touring bicycle, use it once or twice and then, after realizing they aren't going to be doing any more bicycle tours, sell it a few years later for a fraction of the price they originally bought it for.

Before buying any used touring bicycle, be sure to check the bike for major cracks or breaks in the frame and other components. Some parts are more easily replaced or repaired than others.

There are several companies around the world that specialize in custom-made touring bicycles. These bicycles cost much more than the mass-produced touring bicycles and are especially useful to people with physical abnormalities that prevent them from riding a traditionally-sized touring bicycle, or for people conducting unique bicycle tours that require an equally unique bike.

Don't be surprised if you go into your local bike shop and find that the person working there wants you to buy a bicycle that isn't specifically designed for bicycle touring (usually offering you a road or hybrid bicycle instead). Some bike shops simply don't know about the intricacies of touring bicycles. Others are simply trying to make a quick buck by selling you their current inventory, rather than doing the work necessary to get you the bicycle you truly want and need.

Finally, if you have any questions about finding the touring bicycle of your dreams, be sure to contact me with the special $25 value coupon in the back of this book and I'll gladly answer any question you might have.

Are You Ready To Find Your Touring Bicycle?

So, there you have it! You've learned about the unique features found on most touring bicycles; you've learned about the different types of bicycles tours; and we've discussed the five main types of touring bicycles.

You've learned everything you need to know before purchasing a new touring bicycle.

Now the next step is to discover exactly which touring bicycles are available to you in your part of the world.

In the free supplement that comes with this book you will find a large collection of touring bicycles in all different shapes, sizes, colors and designs, from both large and small companies all across the globe.

To find your ideal touring bicycle, simply decide which category of bicycles you wish to search through (whether it be Commuting, Sport Touring, Light Touring, Road Touring or Off-Road Touring bicycles), flip to that section of the supplement, and then go through the list of bicycles in that category to find the one that best suits your needs.

To download this free touring bicycle supplement (as well as two additional bonus items (*A Buyer's Guide To Bicycle Touring Panniers & Trailers* and a 68-minute long video about touring bicycles), just go to the following web address:

    ↗ **http://bicycletouringpro.com/blog/touring-bike-bonus**

Once there, you will be asked for a password.

Your password is: **touringbikes747016**

After entering your password and clicking the "Submit" button, follow the instructions on the following page to download the bonus items.

You will need *Adobe Reader* installed on your computer, tablet or smartphone device in order to access these free bonus documents. You can download *Adobe Reader* for free at the following web address:

    ↗ http://get.adobe.com/reader/

If you run into any problems downloading or accessing these free bonus gifts, send an email to contact@bicycletouringpro.com with your name, password, and what exact problem you are experiencing and someone will get back to you shortly.

Learn More About Bicycle Touring

The information contained inside this book is only an intro to the basics of bicycle touring.

If you wish to learn about some of the more advanced techniques, strategies and challenges of long-distance bicycle touring, I recommend you pick up a copy of my book, *The Bicycle Traveler's Blueprint: The Definitive Guide To Self-Supported Bicycle Touring.*

The Bicycle Traveler's Blueprint contains some of the most detailed and easy to understand information on bicycle touring anywhere in the world.

The book is divided into three main sections.

- ⊀ Chapter 1 describes what kind of gear to use and what to pack for a bicycle tour of any length.

- ⊀ Chapter 2 discusses the planning and preparation process.

- ⊀ Chapter 3 delves into what first-time bicycle tourists should expect once they hit the road (both mentally and physically).

The Bicycle Traveler's Blueprint has helped thousands of people from all around the world conduct their own bicycle touring adventures and it can help you too!

Learn more here: **www.bicycletouringbook.com**

Or visit the address below to see all the other bicycle touring resources that are available to you: http://bicycletouringpro.com/blog/resources/

Still Have Questions?

If you have a specific question you would like to ask me about finding your perfect touring bicycle, please don't hesitate to get in touch.

The best way to reach me is via email: contact@bicycletouringpro.com

While I receive hundreds (sometimes thousands) of emails every day and am often times traveling by bike myself (and away from a computer), I do my best to quickly answer any emails I receive. While a reply may not always be prompt, I will respond to you if you send me an email and ask me a short, logical question.

Thanks for reading... and I wish you much success on your future bicycle touring endeavors.

Printed in Great
Britain
by Amazon